And Say What He Is

And Say What He Is
The Life of a Special Child

J. B. Murray
and Emily Murray

The MIT Press
Cambridge, Massachusetts, and London, England

A portion of the royalties from sales of this book will go to the Denver Children's Hospital.

This book was set in IBM Press Roman
by Technical Composition
printed on Finch Title 93
by The Colonial Press, Inc.
and bound in Columbia Milbank Linen MBL 4647
by The Colonial Press, Inc.
in the United States of America.

Library of Congress Cataloging in Publication Data

Murray, John B
  And say what he is.

  1. Mentally handicapped children—Personal narratives. I. Murray, Emily, joint author. II. Title. RJ506.M4M87   362.3′092′4 [B]   75-5810
ISBN 0-262-13115-3

Contents

Preface

This is the story of a child who had no words to say what he was. It has been for us a story that must be told. The life it records took place, in a sense, outside and beyond the usual measures of time. But days are where he lived, and we have chosen to tell his story in the words that are closest to those days. We begin with the threads of another story, which preceded and prepared the way for his.

We offer this telling in a spirit which we hope corresponds with his spirit, as we knew it. Not everything will be explained, or canceled, or connected, because in him it was not. We have left out the historical and professional present that affected our lives but had little relevance to his. The form is as close as we can approach to this child's spirit, which was benign, coherent and cohesive, an element of blinding joy, a discipline and a measure, an abundant bough, a source, a confirmation, and a revelation.

The original records from which we have worked were produced first out of habit and circumstance—the letters from the accident that our families were living on separate continents, the diaries from a habit of putting things down. Later, when these writings proved of diagnostic value, they were continued as observations of his activities and capacities. Finally, when the clinical picture ceased to matter in any practical sense, the habit was steadier and filled a deeper need. It became an outlet and a relief, a way of not forgetting, of saving as much as could be from all that must be lost. Its measure was not of his progress but of the pulse of his spirit, and of ours.

The voices heard in this book are mainly our own—his parents'. Usually the context or content will make clear which of us is speaking; where there is any doubt, it will be found not to matter. The narrative bridges, and the poems and fragments of verse in italics, are nearly all the father's. Asterisks mark a change of speakers within a single day's entry. The reports from doctors that we have included, though presented at the time they were written, were of course not seen by us until much later. The names we have given them and the other persons in the story may or may not be their real ones.

There are so many people we should thank for help with this book, and this life, that we cannot name them here. Many—by no means all—appear in the text. Our only present expression of gratitude must be in the dedication of this volume to all of them, and especially to Rosalie.

J. B. and Emily Murray

Prologue

1961

FOR THE BIRTH ANNOUNCEMENT

I put behind me that dark territory,
That long sleep and dream.
O sun, world, and air—
I am here!

9/23

To Dr. Thomas's office, all empty on a Saturday morning.
He flashes us the ghostly X-ray image, a skeleton like a
hound, crouched. "Anencephalic"—a failure of the upper
skull to develop. "Incompatible with life."

"You will have to decide if you want to try again. Lightning usually doesn't strike twice in the same place, but
sometimes it does."

9/25

I was dreaming that it would not be so bad. The baby was
born and I saw it. The skull bone was incomplete, but
everything else was all right. When I woke, Emily was crying. It gets worse.

Long-distance calls. My aunt Mani phoned from Santa
Monica, our nearest family. Our friend Norma wanted to
come right over from Pasadena, and did. "Of course you
will have more babies." She had asked her doctor, who had
done some research on anencephalics, and he said we should
have every chance for a normal baby. Half the grief would
be done away with if we don't have to think we will not
only lose this one but never have a chance at another.

10/5

To the obstetrician's again, no sign of labor beginning, and
after, to the mortuary to make arrangements. On the way

home, we stopped to see the cemetery, a small public one between some vegetable gardens and the railroad tracks.

10/9   Cables to Scotland and New Zealand: STILLBORN IN-FANT GIRL BORN MONDAY NIGHT EMILY WELL DELIVERY NOT DIFFICULT FONDEST LOVE JOHN

10/10   A woman in a light-brown uniform came to Emily's room with a Certificate of Fetal Death for me to sign. Printed in big capitals were the Causes of Death: (1) PROLAPSE OF CORD. (2) BREECH POSITION—FOOT FIRST; and, under Other Causes or Complications: ANENCEPHALIC MONSTER. A technical term.

Oct. 12
9:45 A.M.   Two telegrams from New Zealand: GOOD GIRL and MOTHER PASSED PEACEFULLY AWAY THIS AFTER-NOON THURSDAY

Sat.,
Oct. 21   I think I weep so for Mother because there was so much imperfect in her, and in me, and in our relationship. I wish I could wipe out everything I did that displeased her and also wipe away all that hurt me in her. I think I weep for the harshness of human experience, in which love is often possessive and imperfect, demanding what it cannot have, and yet how I wish I could have given what she wanted. And I weep to think that in these past nine months while she was dying there might have been any little thing I could have done to bring her pleasure that I did not do. And now I must rest, for I am weeping for myself.

Sun.,
Oct 22   Consolations? Our nurse friend Minna came for a walk with us. Clear golden day. She had talked to the pathologist, who said that the autopsy showed no other defects—which is very good, since it means the damage occurred at one

3 The Life of a Special Child

time, and probably from some clear, specific cause. Other defects would suggest continued damage throughout pregnancy, which might mean I was responsible—the uterine environment I provided.

Oct. 23 An official representative of the Faculty Wives arrived this morning with some flowers. Pompey-Dog tried to rape her—leaped across my sofa bed at her. She took that all right, but when she said she hoped I would soon get involved in Faculty Wives affairs, and I replied I didn't know what I would be doing—I might take a job, since we had had these medical expenses and would have to save up for the next baby—she became very nervous, saying she hoped I would keep up my "good attitude."

I responded, "I don't know when we will have another baby, though perhaps fairly soon."

She became even more nervous and said, "You usually have to wait a year." Just then a child of hers wandered in, and she grabbed it (as if we were contagious?) and dashed off.

Fri., A friend from the East. *Her* consolation, to tell us of a
Oct. 27 couple who lost *two* babies and then had six healthy children. And when we mentioned that ours had been a girl, her reply, "Next time it will be a boy. Who wants a girl to start off with anyway?"

Yesterday the young woman from across the street, who had never spoken to us before, called out to me, "What did you have?" At first I didn't catch what she meant, so she added, "A boy or a girl?" What do you say? *Neither.*

Saturday, *BY WAY OF ELEGY*
November 18

You are not even a small black box in the lost-luggage room of memory,

4 And Say What He Is

Nor a brief bare spot of ground: the grass has grown over
already;
Nor a remembered cry; nor something darkly snapped
against the eye;

But a sunken bulge in your mother's belly, and now her
untasted
Tears of thick bright yellow milk all wasted.
The bill for only thirty-three dollars for arrangements is
returned marked "PAID."

Who we were, where we came from, what we were doing—these are
natural questions. At the time of the stillbirth we were both about thirty.
Emily, who had come to America as an exchange student from New Zealand, had been teaching at a state college in Southern California while
I studied for my Ph.D. nearby. We had met and married when we both
were graduate students in English. At the start of the summer of 1961 we
had moved from the inland heat and smog to the cool of the coast, where
I was starting my first teaching job.

This move had taken us out of a small college town where we had many
friends to a city where we knew only one or two families. And there we
were, when the stillbirth closed one set of our plans. I had my job, but
Emily had lost not only her child but her mother, not only her occupation but her colleagues and friends, and, for most of her days, she was
alone in a bleak new subdivision, with no car, and no one to call on.

In the spring she was unexpectedly offered the chance to teach for six
weeks at a small private school. She enjoyed it, her spirits were lifted, we
began to make friends, and at the end of the school year we felt ready to
undertake another pregnancy. Also, my dissertation, still being worked
on, began to gather momentum in the summer months. Then in August
we found the house we had been searching for, among avocado and lemon
groves on an old ranch, with a heavy oak on the front lawn and a barn
owl nesting in a big palm. It seemed sufficiently wild and seasoned: termites would swarm from the woodwork in spring, and raccoons would

tramp at night through the dried avocado leaves like heavy-footed burglars.

Within these natural surroundings the whole cycle of birth and death took on a special nearness. Some of the things we saw were benign and amusing—the seals we swam out to greet from the nearby beach, or the geese our landlord decided to raise, which would litter our lawn with their droppings like bright green cigarettes. Others appeared malevolent—the owl droppings on the lawn full of crunched-up mouse bones, or the scene one night in October, when I watched my window spider catch and wrap up a large fly, then carry him in a bundle to the top of the frame. He climbed up by two thin strong lines let down between the web and the pane. It was dreadful to watch the fly struggling and kicking even when all wrapped up.

That fall we switched roles in order to hurry my dissertation along: Emily taught in my place at the university, while I read and wrote at home and did the housework. We knew that keeping busy would help us not brood on our chances. We could not feel the innocent radiance of our first pregnancy, but we held instead to a firm purposefulness and informed hope. Our obstetrician, whose kindness and wisdom had helped us weather the first birth, declared as soon as he could be certain—even without an X ray—that the baby's head was normal. The birth was due sometime in March of 1963.

1963

In the first week of the new year, my father died in Edinburgh. With my older brother, Peter, I flew to Scotland to attend the funeral and to help our younger brother, Douglas, settle the estate. At the crematorium, a platform lowered the coffin silently away. Afterward many of my father's friends, silent Scotsmen I had never met, shook hands with the three sons and turned away into the bright cold sunlight.

This death left the coming baby with only one surviving grandparent, his mother's father in New Zealand. During the Second World War, my father, who had retired to California after a career in British India, had taken a job in a more severe climate and left me, since I had been a sickly child, in the care of my aunt and uncle in Southern California. So Mani—the Indian nickname had been given to her by my father—though she was an aunt only by marriage, had largely taken my mother's place for the next six years, and again after 1955 when my parents returned to Scotland. Then, after my mother died four years later, it was to Mani that Emily stood in the often uneasy relationship of daughter-in-law. My older brother had lived in Mani's house even longer than I and had now settled near her with his family.

The only other "family" we had in this country was Fran, a much younger woman than Mani, recently widowed and the mother of two grown children, but she was related to us not by kinship but by love and loyalty. She and her husband had made themselves Emily's first real friends in America, after being her hosts during a foreign students' tour. She had also stood in for Emily's mother at our wedding. From her home in the foothills of the Sierra Nevada near Sacramento she had flown south to help us through the agony of the stillbirth, and she would fly down again when the new baby was born.

February 26   I dreamed that the baby was born alive but it had an un-
naturally small head, sort of half-anencephalic. I took him

7 The Life of a Special Child

into my arms with tears in my eyes.

March 2   Tonight we sat by the fire, and John read me what he had
been writing. When he came to the lines about the first
baby, I felt a rush of tears but also a lifting of a weight,
exorcised by the words.

*

RHAPSODY: IN THE HABITATION OF DRAGONS

And the parched ground shall become a pool,
and the thirsty land springs of water: in
the habitation of dragons, where each lay,
shall be grass with reeds and rushes.

                                        Isaiah 35:7

While listening, tonight, to a clear music
Partly familiar, but also partly strange,
A silence gathered among us like a small pool,
As clear as tidal water, as near, as particular,
The size and shape of our small Indian hearth rug
And equally shot with gold, green, rose, and blue:
In the habitation of dragons, at the door of the desert.

This silence had no long hands. It wore a gleam;
Like honey it swept through us. It lay down
In the rushes of the rug. I saw it settle a minute,
But only a minute, before it lifted its wings.
And now while I dream or read of Indian serpents
Which break their shells and die, all outside becomes
*   inside—*
I could not say it quicker or more quiet—

The familiar becomes strange, the old becomes the new:
As this morning I polished the old brass switch-plates white,

And my father's and mother's bowl of soft Indian silver
Now melts with sweet light in a pool of silence like grass;
And the child unknowing, concealed in our hopes, so
  swollen
Full, to break out so soon into our listening
That already we seem to hear him, becomes now urgent

To breathe. Today, rewriting the old words
I wrote when our first child neither lived nor died
(But as it were an after-dinner's sleep), I cried—
But only (as it were) outside and in words.
Tonight in this silence I describe there is no crying,
In the strange familiar music where the silence lies,
In the tides or rushes and flowers of the Indian rug.

The seven lucky stars have not faded. The thirsty ground
Drinks, where the dragons depart their old habitations.
The tide not only alternates, it alters.
That pool of silence I was talking about—it fills,
It gathers its waters as to the sea of waters,
In its pureness, as if Jesus had blessed it, it rises,
Its wings are of gold, its deepest griefs are healed.

**Monday,
March 4**

The due date. Visit to Dr. Thomas. Every time he feels it, he says, "That's a good head."

"It won't be born before midnight."

"It'll probably be this week."

**Monday,
March 11**

The waiting continues. Irregular contractions all day. To Dr. Thomas in the afternoon—"It could be any time." A contraction crossed Emily's abdomen. "That's hard as a brick."

Martha, who now cleans house for us one morning a week, says, "If it's late, it's a boy. Women are full of curiosity." An old Italian saying. Is it tonight? The moon is one night

9   The Life of a Special Child

past the full. It seems to say *tonight,* warm and large to the east.

9:30 P.M. Drove to the hospital, after phoning Dr. Thomas. Very hot in the building.

10:00 P.M. Dr. Thomas arrives in a fur-collared trench coat. To me: "Hello, my friend. You nervous? Nothing to be nervous about." He strolls at a leisurely pace along the corridor to see Emily, then in a flash pops out of her room, already taking his coat off. Halfway up the hall, turning into the nurses' station, he sees me standing anxiously and calls back, "Patience."

11:42 P.M. She was whisked away on the cart to the elevator and up to the delivery rooms a minute ago, having just begun the final bearing-down stage. I stayed with her through the last hour, roughly. The rough was *hers*—the big contractions actually tossed her from side to side.

11:55 P.M. Two men and a woman are waiting in this room with me. Every time the elevator door opens, right across the hall, we all lean forward to look. One man's wife was in labor all last night as well as today, like Emily last time.

It will soon be tomorrow, and when it is, our lives will have changed completely.

And Say What He Is

1963

Doctor Thomas said, "Open your eyes and see him born,"
and as the shoulders slipped through, the baby cried, a
great hearty yell, to my astonishment. A nurse told me
this was the sign of a healthy baby. The doctor looked him
over quickly and exclaimed, "He's all right, he's perfect!"

I lay quiet and peaceful, not really very tired, while he
cleaned up. They untied me, slipped me onto a gurney,
and wrapped me in warm blankets—I had the shakes by
now—and put the baby by my side. I had watched him in
the crib, raising his right arm up and down. Now here was
this funny little creature with so much hair on his head, in
my arm. Dr. Thomas was so jubilant you would have
thought he was the grandfather!

*

8:00 A.M.

Began the phone calls—Mani first, very excited that it's a
boy; Fran, all choked up. Cables to Scotland and New
Zealand: JOHN JAMES ARRIVES   EMILY WELL. Only
once did it occur to me how happy my father would have
been at the news.

When I saw young John at noon today, I confess I wasn't
dazzled by his beauty! He has a wide face, lots of fat, his
color is unexciting. But he has long, fine fingers, and his
hair is wild like a poet's. He looks unusual; he stands out
from the others. "A British baby," Emily says.

I haven't *touched* him yet, and that's one trouble. I can't
believe it until I do. But soon, soon, very different. I think
he will become—I think before very long—my friend, "my
son John."

There is a new person in the world today.
I have given him a name, but that is not his name,
He must make it, his own, and be what he says he is,
And say what he is. And if he is my son,
That is not what he must become.

Thursday,
March 14

Visited Emily and John James briefly. As I held him, the first time, tensing, he cried, and I thought, "He'll never love me!"

Friday,
March 15

An older friend once warned me, "Don't worry if you don't love the baby right away. It's looking after them that makes you love them." And it's true! At first I was absorbed with my own part in the drama of birth. Only when they brought his crib to my room and left him in reach of my hand, to care for, did my feelings flood toward him.

Much excitement around us in Obstetrics. Nurses who had tended me for the other baby kept dropping in, day and night, to see me and offer their congratulations.

When I was wheeled out of the hospital, Fran was waiting. We both burst into tears, the baby in my arms, wrapped in his beautiful Shetland shawl, sleeping and serene.

*

5:30 P.M.

They are in the house, both sleeping. Wind from up the coast today, perfect clarity of air, out my window a yellow gleaming light on the grass and weeds. It is unbelievable that he is here. Now he makes a noise—it is a comfort just to hear it, especially the quieter dying-out sound.

March 22

I feel more closely bound to Emily by this child who lies between us in bed at the 5:00 A.M. feeding. A heart beating there which should go on beating past ours, and yet *is*

13 The Life of a Special Child

ours—from us.

To Dr. Howard, our kindly G. P., this morning for the baby's first checkup—"Everything going just fine."

March 25

Another huge mail of congratulatory letters. More presents for the baby, too. Mrs. Allen, who cleaned our house when Emily was teaching at the state college, sent three of the dollars for which she works so hard. I feel bowed, humbled. How can we direct and not waste this precious life?

March 27

Visit by my brother's family—Uncle Peter and Aunt Eleanor, Cousins David and Katherine. They brought splendid presents: a long-handled silver spoon, a crib-size yellow blanket, and a sporty little one-year-old's swimsuit striped in red, white, and blue! Two stiff and awkward brothers, like pelicans. "Uncle Peter"—how good it feels not to be only "Uncle John" forever.

April 4

Time has done a strange thing since this baby arrived—it has disappeared into a primitive world. All is continuum, and exact memory is lost. It seems in a way as if we have always had him, but also it isn't yet quite real.

April 15

[From a letter to the grandfather in New Zealand]
I keep wishing you could see him. It seems so selfish to be enjoying him all by ourselves. He smiles now, such a merry smile. In his bath he is one broad grin. And what a funny little creature he is with no clothes on, his arms and legs going biff, bam, all the time. "A muscle man," John calls him. Martha says he is pretty enough to be a girl! However tired we are at night, the morning is always pleasant, getting up to a new day with him.

April 20

Mani's visit. In anticipation I feared I don't know what. To

14 And Say What He Is

me as a boy she was an impatient woman. But now she is old, and she holds the baby a little awkwardly, as a woman may who has never borne a child. She and Emily stand off, the two main women in my life. They don't know each other well enough for respect to grow between them—probably they are too similar in some ways: "strength of character" and pride. There is only small talk among us, and I feel the immense sadness of things.

Mani loved seeing John James. Told me privately that he looked like me as a baby, "a real Murray." Did not want to offend Emily by saying so in her presence.

June 28   Three months is a blissful stage! The baby uses his hands well now, shakes his rattle, fingers his fingers. Tonight as he was nursing, he started eagerly, then stopped for a few seconds and smiled and smiled at me with his little hands clasped together.

As I was about to put him down, he pressed on his feet, standing, in his crib, and started making steps and laughing louder than I have ever heard. I put him on his back, and he tried to roll over but couldn't. So I put him on his tummy, and he tried to move forward.

We have no name for the baby but "Bubby." A name is needed for other people to use, but we haven't been seeing enough of other people to have to supply one.

July 9   [From a letter to a friend from graduate school]
The joys of country living I don't have time to spend the day chasing geese I am already worn out just trying to do the dishes and get meals and look after Bubby and I can't even get the place vacuumed to keep the fleas down and we haven't even had the dog for six months and here are these damned geese honking outside the door and Bubby is crying because now he is a big boy and needs company

15   The Life of a Special Child

and "judicious stimulation" as Gesell puts it and hell it's
lunchtime anyway.

ADVICE TO A FOUR-MONTH-OLD SON

July 12

My son, if I could advise
you to your occupation
(lying there in the crib
plying your delicate, rapturous hands),
I would recommend medicine—
the healing touch of the physician,
whose brain is bound to his fingers
along threads of nervous balance,
precisely tuned.

And for a hobby, learn
to build any thing of beauty
you can put your hands on: not,
for love's sake, those painterly
flat canvases we pretend
can picture this bumpy world,
nor poems, the same—flat, scratched,
nothing to clasp—no words,
no sounds, no voices.

No, may you learn to cure
by sure touch, giving out
no medicines but the voice,
so healing may flow from your fingers
like smooth ink slowly onto soft ivory pages
from the wise pen of an imagined sage.

August 25

The baby is still very sensitive to noise. When he was tiny
and John scrunched up the noisy cellophane wrapper from
a wheel of Dutch cheese, he screamed in his first real terror.

16   And Say What He Is

Another time, a man's harsh voice made him burst out crying. Now today at our friend's beach house, when the aluminum chairs were dragged across the sandy concrete, he was beside himself. And our dear friend kept on scraping the chairs instead of lifting them. "The thing that gets me about children is they're so irrational," he said! After Bubby has cried very hard, as he did today, he gives great shuddering sobs, even in his sleep, and tosses his head about. I hate to see it.

September 10 Chatting just now with the landlady, who has a grandchild a little older than Bubby. "Isn't he sitting up yet? Why don't you teach him to sit up?" Emily, disturbed and annoyed, cited Dr. Spock on the different rates of development in infancy. As the landlady drove off, I heard a loud flapping among the dry palm fronds and looked up—the owl! I had seen him ghostly the night before last, out the window. He flew from one tree—a "mothlike flight," the *Field Guide* describes it—in a circle and into the other. His colors are white, cinnamon, and buff.

September 13 Took the baby for a six-month checkup to Dr. Howard, who pays so little attention to him that Emily feels uneasy. The pediatrician who took his place last month made a much more thorough examination.

October 8 "Isn't it amazing to have this little Bubby?" I keep asking John. Seven months, and he sits in my lap and smiles at the world. His back is getting straighter, so he may not be too far from sitting by himself. Shakes his rattle, then stops it to see the two marbles spinning round and round inside. Puts his fingers together as if counting them. A great deal of *aah-aahing* these days, a soft sweet sound, back and forth between us.

17 The Life of a Special Child

| October 14 | Visit to Dr. Howard, who checked him over carefully. We are more satisfied. Says we need not bring him in again until January. |
| | Bubby laughed at Martha today when she talked to him—such a quiet, pretty little laugh—but screamed when *she* laughed. |

In November, at the end of his eighth month, the baby had his first real illness—diarrhea that persisted for five days. On the second day there was blood, which frightened us, and one evening he could not be rocked to sleep even though he was desperately tired and weak. His stomach shrank until the skin was as loose as a woman's after childbirth. We had read that diarrhea used to kill babies, and we became anxious about our doctor's unconcern—he didn't even feel he needed to see him. Even when the baby was recovering and our doctor said he was fine again, we found it hard to believe him. Some initial confidence was shattered; we had lost an innocence, and we would be more wary. Another voice had entered the conversation, but it was not Dr. Howard's, so casual and aloof.

At Christmas we drove up to see our family, and we managed the baby's first big visit fairly well. Mani talked to him and played with him on her bed for hours. At first he was nervous with so many strangers. We had still been living a rather isolated life, pushing the dissertation toward a January deadline—a task on which we were both working, I writing and Emily typing—and this had left little time for going out to see people.

Luckily we had found new friends near at hand. Through the avocado grove our landlord had built a small apartment house, and at the start of the school year a new pair of tenants appeared whom we soon got to know. Gerald taught at the university, Amy in an elementary school. We gave them their first acquaintance with a small baby, and they took to him, and he to them, with delight.

Also, late that fall, a graduate student from the university moved into the attic apartment of our landlady's house, and with her we would form a longer association. Like us, Penelope had been born in a British country, and her father, like mine, had worked in India for the British Empire. Like ours, her remaining family was small and scattered. She had worked for international organizations and had lived abroad, and with that background, her Greek name, and her study of foreign literature, she brought to the avocado ranch a certain cosmopolitan charm, which did not, however, conceal an equally charming vulnerability and simplicity. To these qualities Baby John, as she called him, responded warmly, and he provided her an enjoyment that she expressed with all the enthusiasm of a young woman who cannot yet consider having children of her own.

As the year ends, then, Baby John sits contentedly in his bouncing chair, gazing at his toys and spinning his rattles. He is very undemanding for a nine-month-old, and neither his best friends—Penelope, Gerald, and Amy— nor his parents know enough about infants to worry about it.

1964

January 18   Took Bubby for his ten-month checkup. Dr. Howard said we should consult a pediatrician "to see if his not sitting up is normal or not—perhaps with his long back he needs a brace." Very alarming, but when we asked if this was serious, he said no, he didn't think so.

We drove straight from his office to visit our friend Mary. Little John wriggled about very actively on the carpet and was delighted to play with her three-year-old boy. Mary was reassuring, "He's *trying* to move, Emily. He wants to— he's just not ready."

The pediatrician, Dr. Neilsen, was not to see him until the next Tuesday. In the meantime we prepared for his verdict by noting closely all the things our baby could do: how, although he could not crawl, he could propel himself on his back by digging his heels into the rug. Or how, when we carried him, he could shove away from our shoulder with his arms, straightening his back, so that it was hard to keep him from falling. Or how, with the same arching movement, he could lift himself almost out of his infant seat.

Besides, he could do so much with his hands—seize a spoon when he didn't want it and push it away, reach for things on the table and grab them, quickly and decisively—even pinch us. If anything, we supposed, he might be a shade too intellectual, like ourselves; he was delighted when we read to him and turned the pages of his little books. But he seemed to have plenty of physical tricks to show off to the doctor.

Tuesday, January 21   During the examination the baby sat limply on John's lap, his head hanging forward and his jaw slack. I'd never noticed him looking so weak before. We had to describe for

Dr. Neilsen what he could do with his hands, since he could not be persuaded to reach for anything.

While we put him on his back on the examining table to remove his diapers, Dr. Neilsen was collecting his instruments. He came over, glanced at him, and then turned abruptly to us. "Does he always lie with his legs flopped out to the sides like that?" I said no, only for changing his diapers. But now I'm not sure, and if it isn't true, what does this mean? It frightens me. And Dr. Neilsen doesn't seem to know. He said, "We could give all sorts of tests, but usually we come out the same door we went in."

*

[Excerpts from a letter, Dr. Neilsen to Dr. Howard]
The infant is "floppy" in that he is fairly relaxed in being held. He does not sit up by himself; however, he holds his head erect when he is held up. He is alert and responsive, vocalizes somewhat.

When placed on the examining table, he did not turn over, or could not turn over, without some assistance; made crawling movements that were quite in-coordinated. However, he did not show any extraneous or bizarre type of movements that would be associated with cerebral palsy. Throughout the examination he lay on his back in a frog position. Deep tendon reflexes were suppressed in both legs, and the muscle tone seemed somewhat less than average.

I would outline a couple of possibilities. One is that he has what is becoming known as the "floppy infant" syndrome, which has a fairly good prognosis and just seems to represent some delay in maturation of the major motor system. The second possibility is that this is one of the more rare neuromuscular disorders of the Werdnig-Hoffmann-Oppenheim type. There does not seem to be any evidence of major brain damage at the present time. I do feel that a neurological examination by a neurologist would be wise. Until we have further observation, I would be hesitant in making a prognosis.

21   The Life of a Special Child

The next day was like the death and birth of a new life. We began to find that none of us was where we had thought we were. When we had described what the baby could do with his hands, Dr. Neilsen had said, "That doesn't sound like a general retardation." The last two words were like bullets whizzing by; but instead of being thankful they had missed us, we were appalled to discover that we were being shot at.

Despite his partial reassurances, we were much too uneasy to wait out the six weeks Dr. Neilsen proposed until his next observation. An older man like Dr. Howard, he had been known to miss things, perhaps out of kindness and a desire not to believe the worst. We wanted a firmer diagnosis, and we decided to consult another pediatrician, Dr. Eldridge, who had a reputation for missing *nothing*. She was a thin, crisp, domineering woman whose manner on first meeting, in her rather dingy cubicles, was deceptively genial. Years later we would hear horror stories about her overdiagnosing quite ordinary symptoms, and one of the friends who had recommended her would add, "I forgot to tell you, you won't *like* her."

Wednesday,
January 22

To Dr. Eldridge in the afternoon. She says he may be retarded, or have cerebral palsy, or a severe muscular disorder; whatever it is, he is definitely not "normal." "Now you two young people have your own lives to lead. Your marriage is more important." Expecting reassurances, we are told: We should put him away.

A repetition of the agony of 1961, only more drawn out. Coming out, Emily said, "This time I don't believe it."

*

Dr. Eldridge tried to get Little John to do all sorts of things, more than Dr. Neilsen. He cried a lot, and succeeded at very little. She wants him to go for tests to her medical school, where she can arrange for the head of Pediatrics, her old professor, to take his case. When I asked if that was really necessary—Dr. Neilsen didn't seem to think so—

she answered caustically, "Why, he's *way* behind!" Then she sat down and lectured us with a horribly false cheerfulness, in an overconfident tone: "I was visiting an institution recently, and the children were all so happy because there wasn't any competition. They do such wonderful things with them. He would be much better off there."

Everything in our lives is being chopped down ruthlessly. I don't even want to look at Little John. In my imagination I see him already deformed, behaving grossly, his features ugly, and I wish he hadn't been born.

*

But he is so *beautiful*, we think, how could anything be wrong? Yet we have to admit that he is still a baby, while a friend's child whom we saw last week, though only four months older, is already a little boy.

But he is so tiny, and sweet, and so beautiful. Is there to be nothing more? Is all this to grow hard and misshapen?

Thursday, January 23
We feel: Then we will have to lose him—he will leave us before long, either (one almost hopes) by a disease that kills or by a retardation whose demands would be more than we could serve. And that makes us feel distant from him, as if he were already not ours. We tend him joylessly, silently.

This morning I had to tell the chairman of the English Department—whose own boy died of a brain tumor. His eyes immediately sprung water. He urged me not to rely on examinations around here or extended treatments. "They don't have enough of the rare cases and are nervous about them." He also said, "Don't worry, you have a job here."

Spoke to Dr. Eldridge on the phone. She will make an appointment for J. J. to go into the medical school hospital a week from Monday, between semesters so that I can be there. They can run all the tests. And then we will see.

The empty feeling. A dead cavern. Things that have been pleasures—making faces at him while feeding him—we cannot do now because they show up his backwardness; they were pleasures to him four months ago, only more intensely. We feel he has not just halted his development, but regressed. We think it must be—might be?—the sudden onset of some disease. And if so, couldn't it have a sudden cure? Or, at least, a cure?

The three fates that Dr. Eldridge grouped so loosely—retardation, cerebral palsy, institutionalization—each had a distinctive resonance for us. From her New Zealand childhood, Emily remembered how once on a holiday she and her parents had come upon a sad family, camping near them on a remote farm. The father told them how his boy, now adult and quite good-looking but with the mind of a small child, had been injured in an accident, and how the mother had sacrificed her life to caring for him at home; they never went out or had anyone in and were too worn by caring for him to have other children. That sort of devotion, however noble, had seemed mistaken—shutting out life, rather than keeping in touch with it.

As for institutions, in her childhood Emily had heard vague tales—"they beat them, you know"—and later, one that was specific. Her sister-in-law taught nursery school, and in her class was a slightly retarded girl. The mother loved the child and wanted to keep her at home; the father hated her. She was put in a huge custodial "Farm School," where the children though well-fed and clean were left to run about like animals. The mother, a month or so later, persuaded the former teacher to visit the place. Already, she found, the girl had picked up bizarre behavior from the more retarded children, yet her craving for affection amid the bleakness of her surroundings was so intense that she sat on her old friend's lap, clinging to her, the whole three hours of the visit. And when she was leaving, the child could not be consoled. "I couldn't bear to go back," the story ended.

Something like that was our image of an institution for the retarded—not beatings, but neglect and indifference.

For cerebral palsy, however, we had quite a different picture. In her university Emily had known an extraordinary man whose body was severely twisted and deformed by that condition, his movements spasmodic and all but uncontrollable, but with a brilliant intellect, a witty and earthy sense of humor, and a delicacy of personal being that had deeply influenced her own development. He had become totally independent, had gone on his own from New Zealand to Oxford for postgraduate study, had learned to make his way around on a special tricycle, had married, and finally had returned with his wife to New Zealand as a university lecturer. All his handicaps were simply less important than the force of his intellect and personality. From knowing him and others like him in the academic world, we knew that a good mind, caught in a distorted body, could make its own way.

Against the chances of such achievement would be ranged those who reject the handicapped, who wish them put away, out of sight; and foremost among these now was our new pediatrician. Yet through her we had direct access to a first-class medical school, whose specialists might be most able to help our child. We had no choice but to put ourselves in her hands—the force of *her* personality would keep us from ever going back to Dr. Howard or Dr. Neilsen—and they were powerful hands.

Friday,
January 24

Asked Amy and Gerald to drop over last night, as on so many happier evenings. Told them what Dr. Eldridge had said. The room went still. Amy cried. Then we turned to other talk, and the evening was gotten through. They promised to return tonight: evening is the hardest time. Fran phoned—coming down to be with us until we go to the medical school for the tests. She had been wondering why he wasn't sitting up.

Our friends tell us to *hope,* and mention all the cases they know of children sitting and walking and talking late. From the brightness and liveliness of his face they can't believe he's mentally retarded.

25   The Life of a Special Child

Emily phoned Dr. Howard to ask if he thought there had been a change for the worse after the diarrhea in November. He said no. "He's always been on the weak side. It just doesn't show up until after six months." But he never gave us any idea he was thinking like this. Why not? Even now he keeps backing away from our questions.

*

Tonight after dinner John said, "I've had enough of this"— our gloomy silence—and kneeled down on the mat with the baby. With a little urging he got him to arch back and roll over from his tummy onto his back. Bubby loved it! The more he practiced, the more excited he became. Even though this should have been done months ago, it's a joy to see it now. Surely Dr. Eldridge is mistaken. Something's not right, but it's not as bad as she says if he can learn to roll over as quickly as this.

When the baby is on his back, he rests his elbows on the floor, his hands limp like flippers. I'm sure this is recent, he used to move his arms more vigorously and his hands more accurately. When I see these things, I don't know whether to ponder them in my heart, alone, or to tell John.

*

Looking through the photos, we find in some that the left eye seems to be not in focus and to cross in slightly. In many we see indications of muscle weakness that were unnoticed before.

There have been moments when we have wished he might be fatally diseased, feeling that that would be most merciful to him. But that is the counsel of despair.

At first our grief was that of a loss—as if he no longer existed. Since then we have been coming back and realizing he is *not* lost. Even if the mind *were* dimmed, there would still be the light of his spirit.

Monday, January 27

This morning he is clearly calling "Um—mum—mum—mum." It sounds like "Mum-mum." "It can't be really," Emily says, "but it excites me." When she hears it, she runs to reinforce it in some way.

In the last three days he has learned to roll from his tummy to his back. He leans and then falls, realizing he must turn his head at the last minute. The books say this usually happens between five and seven months. He is ten. Does this mean an "IQ" of 70? A "backward" child? We fear it must.

Friday, January 31

Fran has been wonderful, playing pat-a-cake with the Bubbins, singing to him, teaching him so much, the two of them laughing together almost all day. We drew our first breath when John taught him to roll over. We walk now very carefully, but we *do* hope.

We drove to the medical school hospital early on the first Monday in February. For two hours or more we waited with a large crowd of other patients at Admissions, jammed in beside Emergency; when we reached the office, there was no record of an appointment for John James. We were strongly tempted to drive right home, but didn't quite have the nerve. When we were finally allowed up to the Pediatrics wing, we waited around for another long while in the Infants Section for anyone to turn up who knew why we were there. The nurse on duty, alone and overworked, was angry with the world. To us her orders were merely brusque—"Take him in there and wait; I don't have any instructions about him"—but to others she was cruel. Soon after we were temporarily settled, an older woman and a younger one, ashen-faced, appeared at the door, holding a small baby

27   The Life of a Special Child

with a tiny head. "Oh no, not another!" the nurse burst out at them, and then, "Oh, I know *you!* You've been here before. What are you back here for *now?*" "The baby is having her cataracts removed," said the pale young mother.

Our cubicle held six tall steel cribs, and was separated from the neighboring cubicles by glass-topped partitions about seven feet high that screened out only the smallest sounds. One could see and be seen by everyone in the section. From our post we stared at the other babies in the ward and wondered what was wrong with *them.*

At last the doctors reached us. Dr. Meredith, the head of Pediatrics, was at once friendly and informative. A woman in her fifties, she greeted us as a senior colleague who would be interpreting the problem before us in terms of her special knowledge. Her tone was authoritative, not authoritarian; she would respect *our* special knowledge and talk to us as educated human beings. As soon as we met her, we felt ourselves no longer at the mercy of the institution—she even gave us a phone number to call if we needed her. She seemed a person we could trust for her abilities and for the manner in which she would treat us and our child.

Along with her came a young male intern and the young woman resident in charge of the Infants Section. Right away, all three of them would take a crack at examining Little John and questioning us, together and apart. We had brought along our many photographs of the baby, neatly arranged in sequence, and Emily had typed a detailed calendar of all the steps we had noted in his development. We had been scrupulous to include everything that we imagined might be of clinical use. Rarely, the doctors told us, were they provided with such thorough documentation, and we thought therefore that they would quickly arrive at a diagnosis. But the intern warned us, in one of our first interviews, to expect nothing certain: "Pacific State Hospital is full of children who have never been diagnosed."

This intern at first struck us as a bit flippant, but as we came to know him, we saw under his mask. He explained, for instance, what was wrong with the tiny baby we had seen; she was a "microcephalic" or "pinhead." At nine months she was the size of a three-month-old. Eventually she should learn to dress and feed herself, and she would live out her life in an institution like Pacific State with others as badly off, or worse, her brain compressed and imprisoned in her tiny skull. As he spoke of her fate, he sounded hurt by it, as were we.

Our baby stood up to his three examiners well. He reached eagerly for their shiny hammers. He held things for them. He impressed them with his trick of shaking his rattle, stopping it, and studying the beads as they spun inside the clear plastic bulb. He was even willing to laugh for the intern, and all in all he performed better than he ever had for doctors.

Yet out of the preliminary examinations there came no diagnosis, only three possibilities: something wrong in the brain, which would appear in X rays or an electroencephalogram; something in the muscles or nerves, which would be tested in other ways; or the now familiar "floppy baby" syndrome. These sounded less ominous than what we had been fearing, but they carried a rider. "If none of these showed up," Dr. Meredith said, "we would have good reasons for probing elsewhere." The next day they would get on with the tests.

We stayed the night with old friends from graduate school. It was a relief to be out of the hospital, but we could not forget why we were there. Here in this friendly household was a little girl only six months older than our little boy, and she was, we noted, "much more advanced." She walked, she talked, she danced and sang—a normal, bright sixteen-month-old girl. It was she with whom he had to try to catch up.

Tuesday, February 4 8 A.M.

Blood sample. Then we gave him breakfast. Later in the day, electroencephalogram, electromyogram, spinal tap, X rays of skull. He goes out of our hands to be hurt, and we allow it although it is our instinct and duty as parents to protect him from harm. It is for his own good, we try to insist to ourselves.

But I didn't need to wean him, poor little fellow. I could have nursed him here, as they let us come into the ward and stay all day. Sitting in his infant seat on a trolley after lunch, groggy from sedatives. Turning his head from side to side, very pale, so pretty.

The intern alone today, without Dr. Meredith. Cheery, keeping our spirits up. J. J.'s fine motor coordination is good. Only the gross motor coordination is not up to normal. Nerves in muscles—electromyogram—test normal; therefore, "not neurological."

Wednesday, February 5

J. J. was to get no food before his muscle biopsy. He was sedated about noon, so we left. Ate lunch, looked in stores. Brandy in the car before going to meet Dr. Meredith. She didn't arrive right away, and we comforted Bubby. After five when she came. She told us the tests so far were all normal. She tried to look at his retinas, grim-faced we thought, perhaps just tired, but he was too upset with everything and kept crying. Tomorrow she will try again.

The father of the tiny unresponsive baby in the next crib, Tracy, was in to see her today, in work clothes. An intern was telling him all the things probably wrong—her kidney infection may have caused brain damage, her head position is odd, and at six weeks she is still fed only from a dropper. "Oh no, all the men in our family sleep with their heads like that; it's just something in the family. When can we take our baby home? We want to get her home." Such tenderness behind his resistance.

Thursday, February 6

Bubby very weak—refused early milk—but ate a lot of fruit and cereal and perked up almost at once. Our intern came along, casual and well at ease and happy. He's sure there is no general retardation. "When we hear of the anencephalic fetus, we think *Aha!* there must be some connection. Floppy baby, that's all!"

But Dr. Meredith is taking great precautions against overoptimism. J. J.'s head is rather large, so there is a slight chance of hydrocephaly. We phoned Dr. Howard to find what the head measurement was at birth—they needed one other coordinate to tell if it was growing too fast. The two measurements fell at exactly the same point on the curve, a little above the mean and well within normal range. "No hydrocephaly there."

Dear God, as we walked to the car
Across the gravelly asphalt,
An American flag in a breeze
With sunlight through its billows
Was no more bright than our eyes.

*

The father of the microcephalic holds the baby with its bandaged eyes so tenderly, holds it and gazes at it. It is hard to bear.

A gentle, cheerful older aide on the ward today. "That sweet young couple," she says of some other parents, "they want their baby home so much. He's diabetic, but they could handle it at home. It's too bad." She talked of Tracy and the microcephalic baby, and their parents' yearning love for their damaged children.

*

There was still the afternoon to get through. Up in the ward, J. J. was being shown to a group of medical students by a professor who ranks so high he doesn't have to wear a white coat.

Rather late we went down to Dr. Meredith, who wanted to find out if J. J.'s eyes follow objects and move together— "tracking," it's called—a subject on which she is doing special research. As she was getting started, the top opthalmologist arrived—a nice man, but you don't keep him waiting. He got a very thorough look into the eyes and declared them quite normal.

After he left, J. J.'s head was hooked up all over again to electrodes around his temples like a little crown, and he was placed in a barrel within which a paper reel scored with thin and thick black lines revolved. Through the electrodes a graph was made of his eye muscle movements, which showed that his eyes *do* track.

*

As our news gets better, we begin to feel we own the hospital, we know our way around it and are not its victims any more. The intern is elated. They think our Bubby is a sweet little guy, and they want him to pass their tests, too. We offer to help with the other babies. We feel we are escaping, but that does not lessen our pain at seeing the ones who have no hope.

Friday,
February 7

Waiting around for the bill, I looked up "anencephalic" in a textbook on fetuses in the medical school bookstore. Not what one would have wanted to see in person, though there are two degrees of it, a lesser one (like ours) in which only the top of the skull is missing, and a worse one in which that and the whole of the spinal column lie as if split open. In both the ears are thick and the eyes protrude, giving an apelike appearance: it is inadequate to imagine, as I occasionally have, a face like Little John's as he was at birth cut off above the eyebrows. But there are monsters much more terrible. There is a Cyclops, whose two eyes merge into one socket. (The mythological creature then was a projection of what had been seen occasionally in human births?)

I was surprised that these pictures, factual as they are, did not distress me.

February 10   [Excerpts from a letter, Dr. Meredith to Dr. Eldridge]
It is my impression that this child can be placed in the benign congenital hypotonia or "floppy infant" group, but that one has to be a little guarded about the intellectual ability. There is no doubt that there has been significant lack of stimulation, and it seemed to me that before a developmental test in detail is recommended, a period of stimulation should ensue.

The parents were instructed in such a stimulation procedure, which would involve attempts to build up motor strength as well as to develop interest and response in the child. I should appreciate an opportunity to see him again in about three months.

We drove away home as fast as we could with our tentative good fortune. Whatever the validity of the theory of a lack of stimulation, which had been raised because of our absorption in the dissertation, its practical effects demanded that we set to work as parents can when a child's handicap is limited and known, and specific exercises may help. Mental development at this early age is almost inseparable from muscular: if he could not reach the world, we must bring it to him.

With the admission of his weakness had come a sense of purpose. We read what we could in the studies of development, taking encouragement from one specialist who wrote that when a baby smiled on time or early—as ours had—he always had great hope for its mental normality. The books also gave us useful patterns for the baby to learn and practice, and so we pumped his legs and arms to strengthen their muscle tone and stroked his hands to stimulate the nerves. We talked and sang to him and played him records, and we carried him out and around to meet the world.

After the horrors we had glimpsed, we could not but feel that our child had been restored to us and that he had a future, though we did not look too far into it. The present was busy enough, with its games and exercises. In May we were to visit Dr. Meredith again, to report and display his accomplishments. It was an anxious period, full of small but real triumphs, a time for taking and noting short views.

March 4   He has been crying a lot with teething pain, so we took him to Dr. Eldridge in case there might also be another ear infection. We asked her about the tremor we sometimes see in his jaw.
"Neurological."
"Is it serious?"
"We'll see." Her usual cold comfort.
She approves of *switching* a baby's legs to make it crawl faster! "Just get a thin little switch of willow"—unbelievable. She seems more detestable each visit.

March 12   Baby John's first birthday—very different from what we would have imagined a few months ago. Since leaving the hospital and getting over the cold he caught there, he has been moving and vocalizing much more efficiently. He can hold his head steady on command and turn it by himself—lifts it from the mattress, turns toward us, and holds it, calling "Aah" to attract our attention. He can play peekaboo, hiding his face and then lifting it up—gales of laughter, and then he collapses and hides it again. His grip is surprisingly strong, and he has begun to help with his arms as we pull him up from a lying to a sitting position. He lifts his arm and lets it fall, to wave bye-bye.
He can now enunciate quite distinctly "Da" and "Hi Da," with variations and control, though we're not sure if he means his father or not. When he is unhappy, he murmurs "Mum-mum-mum." One day we were going through all the noises the animals make, when at "doggy" he suddenly rolled his head. Since then, whenever we come to "What does the doggy say, John?" he gives his head a roll and laughs.

34   And Say What He Is

Soon after the birthday, Emily's aunt Stella in New Zealand sent us a gift of money. We decided to spend it on a vacation, and drove north to see some old friends—especially Fran, the baby's honorary grandmother. He obviously remembered her from her recent visit, for he lifted his head and kicked his heels higher than for anyone else and laughed more rapturously than we had seen him do before. But he was delighted with everything. We took him to restaurants, where he sat through the meal, cheerful and interested in the comings and goings of waitresses and customers. He went to various houses and met our friends and their children. He traveled well in the car, playing peekaboo from his crib behind the front seat and talking away with earnest *ahs* and *dahs.* It was a very happy time.

April 8   To Dr. Eldridge. J. J. is 30½ inches long, weighs 20 pounds 3 ounces. She checked him over thoroughly and was impressed with his new tricks. As a result she was amiable, for once, and did all she could to make him not mind being there. We are to call him John, not Bubby, because it's more grown-up, and tie him into a highchair to eat, with diapers as a harness.

April 13   Yesterday Penelope asked us over for afternoon tea to meet her mother. Very English. Penelope told Emily she has been having internal pains and has decided to go to the student health center about them. Driving her to the campus this morning, I in my wisdom diagnosed the problem as psychosomatic.

     Tonight she reported that they think it is a cyst, but they are doing tests to rule out pregnancy—which is humiliating since she knows this cannot be the case. If it is a cyst, though, it will require an operation. The uncertainty makes us all uneasy.

April 15   Noticed today that J. J. seemed more floppy. Several times he dropped his head back and cried while being pulled up.

His eyes crossed a lot, and his arms seem really no stronger for all the pushing and pulling we have been doing. He had trouble manipulating his Busy Box and got very frustrated. Tired?

April 21

Took Penelope into the hospital last night—sweet and brave. Her operation was today, and her mother phoned: full hysterectomy, worse than they had feared, and "no chance it is not malignant."

We felt she had entered another world from ours.

April 25

Little John all tight and shipshape today. Turned over from his tummy to his back for the first time. Accidentally, but all by himself!

April 28

Now turns from tummy to back intentionally and without help. It is fully established.

May 9

The landlady's little smug cat-licking smile when I asked her not to charge Penelope her rent if we got her things moved out by Sunday: "Well, she phoned me to say she wanted to keep the apartment for two more weeks."

I, rather desperately, hating to make the emotional pitch: "But she's so ill, no hope for her, and she has so little money."

And the landlady, sweet as steel: "Why, you should always have hope. I have a friend who had a cancer operation a year ago, and he's just fine now."

May 11

Today Little John pushed himself along the carpet, moving his hands forward one after the other. I would hold his knees together, and he would push them and then begin to move his arms. Greatly excited at the sensation of moving, however draggingly, forward.

Saturday night, May 16 With Sarah, my teen-aged cousin visiting from England, I went this evening to the Bowl to hear Peter, Paul, and Mary, folk-style singers. Sat in the topmost row, in front of us two rows of retarded students from a local school. Great enjoyment and responsiveness, bouncing to the beat, clapping "Yeah." Like children, they laughed eagerly, hoping to understand and thereby to be accepted as adults. When Paul made vocal sound effects through the microphone, one said, "Boy, he's a genius," and another, older, perhaps in his forties and dressed in a conservative business suit— from his appearance you would judge him a substantial citizen—repeated with amusement, "That guy's a gen-i–," losing hold of the last syllable. "I know what that word means," said the boy beside him, who looked exactly like one of my university freshmen, a bright young music student; "that word means that a person is really smart"— as if he were answering a teacher in the classroom. The older man kept wrinkling his eyes and creasing his forehead at one of the girls who leaned on the shoulder of the boy on the other side of him. She took no notice.

Several spoke very, very slowly. And of course, making a big old grade-school joke, Peter (or Paul) would go "duh, duh, duh," meaning "I'm a moron!" And astonishingly, for these kids too it *was* a big joke, and they roared. Only one of the group *looked* "moronic"—with thickened lips and ears, open hanging mouth—and he was obviously one of the brightest and had a girl leaning back against his knees from the row in front.

There was much division among them over who would sit by whom, always polite but of intense importance. Alliances seemed to shift even during the course of the evening, one boy getting up in a huff to sit by someone else. They were very conscious of one another and totally unaware of the other people around—who paid them little attention.

37 The Life of a Special Child

Some of the song lyrics were grotesquely beyond their comprehension. Others seemed painfully to point at their limitations: "All men are born equal, as we all believe," or "Hammer out justice," or Bob Dylan's "How many roads must a man go down/Before he's called a man?"

The whole show—raucous sound system, crude musicianship, corny humor, Mary's stagger-kneed sexy half-hints, bumping and grinding off beat—seemed a surrealistic nightmare. Girls sat above us on the retaining wall, bouncing their heels off the concrete right by our heads. But it was the "normal" people who seemed grotesque, not these others. I felt I wanted to be *their* friend.

It was time for the return visit to Dr. Meredith, this one in her outpatient clinic on a Friday afternoon. There, in a high-ceilinged waiting room as indifferent as the receptionists, we waited under a portrait of the philanthropist in whose name the clinic was endowed. Among the others with us was a baby we now recognized as microcephalic, his grandmother holding him and crooning over him. We went out after a while to the glassy hall, where we found more privacy and a swinging door to amuse Little John. Dr. Meredith finally called us in at about six o'clock.

We tried to persuade Little John to go through his paces, but he had had no nap and no dinner, so he just lay and cried. Dr. Meredith was disturbed by his lack of manual dexterity and the poor pincer movement of his fingers. "We'll have to look further," she remarked—which sank our hearts. She still feared some pressure might be building up in the brain, from hydrocephaly or a tumor, though she admitted there was no real evidence for it.

She directed us to go on with his exercises and to add new ones that would make him pay attention to small objects. She wanted to be sure he could see them. Also, she said, we should get different textures for him to touch; plastic toys are bright and pretty and ingenious, but they all *feel* the same, they don't develop a child's tactile awareness. She advised putting him in a small paddling pool; recently she had visited a rehabilitation pool where the children were doing remarkable things with paralyzed or weakened muscles. "He may always have a problem," she concluded, "or what we have may very well be a slow maturation of the nervous system."

We had expected a more favorable report, since we—and even Dr. Eldridge —had been so pleased with all he had been learning. But, we reasoned, he *was* very tired from the long wait. Besides, she had borne down hard on his fine motor coordination—which in February had been praised as completely normal—while our exercising had concentrated on the large motor skills. And maybe we hadn't kept him at it so well recently, with Sarah's visit and Penelope's operation to distract us. If so, we would work all the harder through the summer.

And yet there was one piece of surprising encouragement. Near the end of the consultation we had asked Dr. Meredith a question that had been in our minds all year: Would it be wise for us to have another child? She replied cheerily, "Sure, go right ahead!" Somehow we couldn't quite believe her, and we held off. We wondered, for instance, if she was remembering the anencephalic—and found out later that she was not.

May 29   [From Dr. Meredith's report to Dr. Eldridge]
          I had hoped earlier that perhaps this child's delay in devel-
          opment could be placed purely on the basis of inactivity,
          but believe that this is certainly not true at the present
          time. The child's overall interest and intelligence may well
          not be retarded, but the hand use certainly is. I did not find
          any sensory loss to touch or pin in either upper or lower
          extremities, but development of the pincer motion is great-
          ly retarded, even beyond some of his other developmental
          activities that could be related to the long body and poor
          musculature.

June 10   Drove Penelope to the radiation center for treatment. One
          of the hardest things I have ever done. This being her first
          day, she wanted me to go in with her and wait, and I could
          not refuse. I sat and looked at the patients. I remembered
          Mother's agony and vomiting, when they jerked her in the
          old bed along the corridor, bump-bump-bump on her can-
          cerous spine, to the radiation room in that medieval New

39 The Life of a Special Child

Zealand hospital, and I thought, "I can't stay here, I can't re-live that memory." Then an aide pushed in a wheelchair with a boy of eight or ten, thin arms bandaged, his face pale and drawn from months or years of suffering, and he put his bandaged hands to his eyes and cried out in panic, "What are they going to do to me?" The aide said nothing, and his mother, healthy, young, capable-looking, got up from her chair and came over to him, but also said nothing. I wanted to reassure him, "It won't hurt, it just goes dark, and you don't feel anything," but I couldn't because I didn't know what was going to happen to him. I hated his stupid mother and the stupid silent aide, and I thought I could not bear it if I had to go there again and watch such pain and fear in a child and nobody doing anything to ease it.

June 13   Helping J. J. swim in his new plastic pool. He loves it and splashes eagerly with his arms. It's marvelous to see how much more he moves in the water. With his mouth closed he looks much older. I suppose it is muscle weakness that lets it hang open. He's doing well picking up sugar cubes between finger and thumb. The tiny red candies Dr. Meredith gave us are still too small and frustrate him, but we will graduate sizes until he is able to grasp tiny things.

July 9   *AUBADE OF THE FATHER*

The noises are too
Insistent, who
Could sleep? Who would
Want to that could?
The baby's awake,
The birds break
The light. Their dances
Begin. He bounces

40 And Say What He Is

His crib: bam bam,
"Da da, mum mum."
Darling, come:
Young lovers, unmarried,
May lie abed;
With other lives to run
We greet this sun.

July 15   Drove Penelope to her doctor. She said afterward that he
told her, "If I were in your position, I would do what I
most wanted to do. In my case that would be to go on
practicing medicine. If you most want to go to Europe,
you should go." Then she looked at me and asked, "What
does he mean? Why does he say something like that?" But
she had been told the worst—that she had very little hope
for the future—a few days after the operation. I hedged,
"You should ask *him* what he means." Is it our place to
force it on her? She has been so brave about the pain and
the radiation sickness, but the facts she evades. We will see
her off with her mother to England in a few days.

*

Amy and Gerald left on the twelfth, very sad about going. I
remembered how we had felt on leaving graduate school—
a great wrenching away from our friends—and I thought:
Now we have Little John, we are steadier, like a tripod.

Sunday,   A distressing phone call from Mani about a doctor from
July 26   Vienna, an endocrinologist, who "has done wonders for
people I know." For her peace of mind, would we take
Little John to see him? At her expense. Emily was very
disturbed by the conversation. She had understood he was
here in town, but neither Dr. Eldridge nor Dr. Thomas,

41 The Life of a Special Child

whom we called for advice, had heard of him. I phoned back and told Mani this. "Oh *they* wouldn't know him. He's far above all of them—an international reputation. He's only known to a very few people who can afford to pay his high fees." As I demurred, she said it was up to us. It wasn't her problem—if we were satisfied. But *she* wouldn't be satisfied until she had had six or seven consultations—gone to the Mayo Clinic. She had found the difference "terrifying" between our Christmas and our June visits.

July 30   Odd dream: gloom. A rustling in the palm tree. I thought: The owl is falling down. Down fell a large bird to the ground, then picked itself up and hurried off on its feet. More like a plucked turkey. Not an owl. Followed by two others of equal size. Martha's Italian proverb: An owl in a tree means death will visit the house.

August 2   *THE STRUGGLE*

The child endeavoring to crawl,
Humping, pumping his limbs,
Tensing his back, his neck
Tensed, with every exertion
Nearer to his unknown goal
Yet caught still in his body—
A grub, a caterpillar,
Aiming toward flight.

GRACE NOTE

I lift my new child
up to the sky, he rests
on my breath blown lightly across
the fair soft hairs of his forehead.

42 And Say What He Is

August 10   Visit to Dr. Eldridge. She suggests a "wonder horse" to help him use his feet. "I have a little mongoloid who is doing marvelously with rocking it," she remarks. The analogy stabs us. How tactless she is.

In the middle of August we bought a small house, set among olive and avocado trees, high on a slope some distance from the city, where the climate was drier and warmer. Its air and shadows, the noises of birds, even of cars burning up the steep road and bulldozers clattering across the way, delighted Little John. Its seclusion sheltered him from the everyday childhood infections, which were always hard for him to shake off, and around it there flowed a peacefulness that seemed to remove it from the pressures of ordinary time.

But the summer was busy, first with house hunting, then with moving, and finally with remodeling to make room for a washer and drier. We had less time to spend on Little John's exercises than we intended, and when he was seventeen months, we set off for his appointment with Dr. Meredith with real apprehension. The drive, as in May, tired him, and by the time she was free, he was again in a dreadful state, weary, irritable, uncooperative. "Walk to your car," she told him, using a word for his stroller that he had never heard. But he made steps to it well, held by her under the arms for balance but supporting his own weight and lifting his feet deliberately. Surprisingly, although he kept crying right through the visit, she was less guarded at the end than in May. His hands displayed none of a long list of neurological or muscular symptoms, for instance. And, she said, acknowledging what we always felt, "He's such a lovely little fellow, it's so worthwhile to work with him." As we drove home, we wanted to share this optimism but were afraid to. Had she really seen all his weak points as well as the improvements? Had she seen his fingers curl? Emily wondered.

September 2   [From a letter to the grandfather in New Zealand]
First of all, we have had a very good report on Little John. Dr. Meredith's conclusion was that he definitely is just a hypotonic baby—lacking muscle tone; no other symptoms

43   The Life of a Special Child

of bad things have shown up. This time she said she would "go out on a limb" and say—although you can't predict absolutely—that she thinks he will outgrow this weakness and have no physical difficulties at all. As for the mental aspect, she repeated that she has never thought there was any problem there. In fact, in one respect he seems rather ahead. We had told her he loves to watch shadows and will raise his head up and down to see his shadow move. She asked if we had shown him the shadows; we told her no, he had noticed them himself and worked it out. It seems this is unusually early for a baby to be aware of shadows, so we were very happy to have some positive sign of his mental ability, since he doesn't talk at all yet; and we came home quite elated.

She told us of a place where we could have a posture jacket fitted for John James, which we now have. It gives a firm support for his trunk, like a corset, with rings to which you can attach clips and hook him securely into a car seat, or into his highchair, or he can dangle from a special rig this man also made which hangs on springs from a sliding garage-door track bolted to a beam. So now Little John can be in a standing position, supported, and touch his feet to the ground and, by pushing slightly, bounce up and down and move himself along with his own steps. This will help him learn to stand by himself, and later to walk, and it will be a great help to me, as he is very heavy now to support in a walking position—almost thirty pounds!

The man who made the jacket was sympathetic and seemed to know a lot about these problems. The vision and the mind's interpretation of it don't develop properly from a prone position; standing in the jumper will help Little John's brain as well as his muscles. He told us he used to accompany Dr. Meredith up and down the state to public clinics for children, she diagnosing and prescribing, and he then measuring and making and fitting the braces and other devices. He sounded very proud and fond of her, and it pleased us to hear this confirmation of our trust.

We now have to go on working very hard with J. J., as Dr. Meredith said that at this stage, if left to himself, he wouldn't just stop progressing, he would go back.

Exactly at the autumn equinox, as classes were resuming at the university, a large brushfire began to burn along the foothills. Although it was five miles off, Emily at once felt nervous and started packing up; our narrow green acre was half-surrounded by dry wild chaparral. And she was right. On the second night we were ordered to evacuate. Friends helped us move out a good load of our basic possessions, and we departed in two cars after midnight, not sure if we would ever return to this house we had hardly lived in yet.

On a ridge near the ocean we paused and looked back. All across the valley, as on some ancient battlefield, watchfires were burning, and each was a house. The wind blew the flames great distances until they caught on a likely structure or tree, and it was blowing hard in the direction of our house. On the third day of the fire we moved out all our possessions—everything we had moved *in* just five weeks before—and that night the fire stood at the top of our road, waiting for the hot fierce winds to whip it down as on the two previous nights. But the winds held off, and our house was safe.

Slowly we hauled ourselves into it once again, our strength and will depleted by these weeks of effort and confusion. We continued to find it hard to keep Little John's exercises going consistently. And he too seemed tired, performing them sometimes in a joyless, mechanical fashion, instead of with his usual exuberance. There were times when he would be screaming more wildly than before, and we would quarrel over whether, and how, we should "discipline" him. Still, we were often joyful, and he seemed to keep increasing in awareness and responsiveness.

October 30   *AFTER A BRUSHFIRE: CODA*

Asleep, he sprawls on the floor,

45   The Life of a Special Child

a prone warrior, stuffed
with his dinner, and no nap.

The sunset melts on the shield
of the bronze-flattened ocean,
the dishwasher churns and disgorges,
and, on the phonograph, soft songs
of lullaby and gentle lambs
have sung the man to sleep:

a center to arcs of chaos,
he slumbers at the hurricane's eye.
Off with him to his crib—

as if he were a grown person
who had swallowed too much wine
and dizzily sung high glees

after the first, soft rains
had drifted, draining into
the cinder-seeded soil.

November 11 [From a letter to the grandfather in New Zealand]
Little John is now bouncing in his jumper. He's
getting more lively in it all the time and last night at bedtime just kept jumping and jumping his feet with such
energy that we let him continue because he is not often so
vigorous in the daytime. He is learning to use his hands
to pull with; we set an armchair in front of him, and he
pulls himself over to grab the arm. The jumper is a marvelous
gadget and helps him balance his head in a standing position.
He is beginning to look like a real little boy now.

November 29, Fran here. We drag around, still tired from the moving and
Thanksgiving
weekend remodeling and the fire. Fran has cleaned up a lot of the
house for us. Little John unsmiling, won't look at her. She

is disappointed, not making much fuss over him. Is it moodiness in him? Fear of the new?

*

An argument with Dr. Eldridge. She spoke of John James as "retarded." But Dr. Meredith never said that, I objected. "She did to me." But he's making progress! "Not as much as we hoped for." Furious with her, I called Dr. Meredith, long distance. "No, Mrs. Murray, you haven't misunderstood me. I have never said he is retarded. I saw a baby recently, now two years old and doing very well, that at nine months seemed quite hopeless. Even if I had thought that, I never condemn a baby until we are sure. If you treat them as retarded and they are not, irreparable harm will be done." She offered to take over all his specialized care, leaving Dr. Eldridge only for colds and sicknesses. But she thinks a developmental test is necessary now, in view of "this other opinion."

November 30   Visit from a graduate school acquaintance, with her little baby, so full of herself and it—the breast feeding, the natural childbirth, even the damned conception!—and so smug about getting herself married off and pregnant that she could hardly listen or notice *at all* about Little John. "Oh," she said, "you wouldn't want to tell your family about him, would you?"

December 5   *A COINCIDENCE*

I dropped my pencil. It broke on
the asphalt floor,
I flung it behind me, ascending,
and through the door

47   The Life of a Special Child

I stepped inside and sat in
the easiest chair,
and reading George Eliot's Middle-
march *pleasantly there,*
I tripped on a sudden passage:
in the minister's jar
a "lovely" (that was his word) "anen-
cephalous monster."

Having glimpsed it dimly across an
X-ray plate
like the New World in ancient maps
still incomplete,

and skillful in tapping the spines
of all the nine
moons of a musing, I turned a
dog-ear down,

and snatched up another pencil
to slash that shape
that lifted above the paper its
crown of an ape,

till once again it would drop,
dripping and warm,
into the cemetery of Hope
its lovely form.

December 7   [From a letter to the grandfather in New Zealand]
    Just a short note to accompany these photographs for
Christmas. Little John sits up well in his highchair, as you
can see, and if he slides over now, it is all in one piece, so
his spine shows more strength. He loves to feed himself and
bang with his spoon on the highchair tray and also to bend
over and smile at himself in its shiny surface. He enjoys sit-

48   And Say What He Is

ting in his car seat and playing with its little steering wheel and honking its horn, while we sing Woody Guthrie's "Let's go riding in the car-car," and "I'm going to let you blow the horn," at which he laughs and holds his head up. He does seem reluctant to use his hands for holding on. Instead he uses his shoulders to keep his back upright in the car seat, and will take his hands away from the crossbar rather than support himself by them.

We do work rather in the dark with him, since nobody really knows why his muscles are weak or what to expect in the way of development. As he gets bigger, explaining him to strangers becomes a bit harder. In a shop the other day he lay limply with his head on John's shoulder, the way we always carry him, and the clerk said, "What a tired, sleepy boy." We started to explain and then gave up. It is all so complicated, just as his many different kinds of exercising—leg raising, arm raising, rolling over, jumping in the posture jacket, picking up little things with his fingers— all add up to a complicated daily routine. But he's so gentle and sweet, and his happiness at every achievement continues to be our chief joy. We will have a nice Christmas tree for him, lots of bright colors to stimulate his sight, and all kinds of manipulative toys for him to work with.

Much as the first pediatrician to see him had predicted, Little John's tests had led us out virtually the same door we had gone in, and the year itself seemed to end where it had begun, with Little John nearly but not quite sitting, crawling, and talking. But there was one big difference: we knew now there was trouble. And we thought there was hope.

1965

Sunday, January 3

Sat above the barranca, listened to the dry sycamore leaves in moving air.

The terms *genius* and *moron* distinguish nothing of importance. On the phonograph, Vivaldi's *Four Seasons;* beside me, Little John bangs at his xylophone with a wooden hammer. Both make music, and it is the same music.

Acknowledging that this is so, one is first appalled. And then—one continues to make or hear whatever music, and the echo dies away.

Wednesday, January 6

Penelope and her mother have returned rather suddenly from England. Traveling was becoming difficult; Penelope is not well. After dinner with us she felt so ill she had to lie down on our bed. The chemical treatments in London have failed.

Thursday, January 7

Noticed today that Little John's hand seems to waver as he takes his spoon to his mouth at meals. Or am I wrong? I'm sure he didn't do this before?

We go to the medical school again tomorrow. He has been crying a lot the last three weeks, and it seems as if all he does is lie on the floor and chew his rattle, not reaching for toys. Yesterday I felt cross and desperate. I'm not built for this slow training and teaching. I don't have the patience to see progress. I feel weary.

When we arrived at the medical school, Dr. Meredith was away, sitting in on the Ph.D. orals of a former patient, a young man with cerebral palsy who had been completely helpless when he was first brought to her as a child. We went downstairs for Little John's developmental examination, and when we came back up, she was in her office, very cheerful: her young man had passed.

Ours we feared had not, and he lay now on her table, and later on her couch, horribly amiable, doing nothing, just smiling. Suddenly she grew very serious. "It's not a question of whether he will make progress," she said. "He'll do that. But it is a question of how far. We'd better have some more tests." And she arranged for him to come back on January 25, during the semester break. We drove home in almost total silence.

January 8   [Report by a doctor from the medical school]
DEVELOPMENTAL EXAMINATION
Name: John James Murray
B. D.: 3/12/63
Age: 22 months
Date: 1/8/65

1. John is placed seated on his mother's lap at the table. The book is presented. He reaches out and hits at the book with his fisted hands, at times possibly giving a small rhythm to his tapping. I do not see any clear evidence of his giving specific attention to parts of the pictures. He occasionally looks at the examiner. He has an obvious strabismus [crossed eyes]. At times it seems he also has nystagmus [spasmodic involuntary motion of the eyeball]. Several times he is very quiet and solemn, but then he smiles after a time.

2. The first cube is presented. He opens his hand partially and takes it. He seems to use his right hand more than his left when doing this. He also carries the cubes to his mouth. He at times holds one in each hand and then will tap them together when he is holding them. He needs a great deal of support from his mother while he is seated in order to maintain himself. His head droops forward on his chest. However, when he is interested in doing so, he seems to be able to raise his head up into an erect position. The head does not bob. The massed cubes are given to him, and he disorders them, picks them up, bangs them around, drops them on the floor.

3. When the cup is presented, he looks at it and bangs at it. A cube is placed into the cup by the examiner. He then bangs at the cup several times, but then reaches in and

51   The Life of a Special Child

touches the cube with his hand, takes it out, carries it to his mouth and drops it. He then picks up another cube and drops it into the cup, reaches in, picks it out, and drops it onto the floor. On several occasions when he is asked to give something to the examiner, it is not possible to tell whether he is responding specifically to this, although he does remove a cube from his mouth and drop it onto the floor.

4. When the bell is presented, he takes it by a junctional grasp and bangs it against the table. When the pellet is presented, he does not seem to notice it. When the bottle is presented, he reaches for it but only occasionally secures it. He does not give any specific regard to the pellet inside the bottle. He is placed supine on the examining table. He lies there quite passively.

5. When the ball is rolled toward him, he brushes at it as if to push it away, but it is quite a passive approach to the toys. He smiles and laughs when someone plays with him in this manner, however. He lies without rolling over or moving on the couch for at least 15 minutes. When the dangling ring is presented, he reaches up for it with both hands. He secures it after a time. When he has secured it, he transfers it from hand to hand and carries it to his mouth. He frequently opens his mouth very widely and puts most of the fingers of his hand into his mouth.

6. At a later time, while he is seated in his mother's lap and has seemed to regain some of his composure, he is induced by the examiner to put three cubes into the cup by handing the cubes successively to him. He then becomes quite fussy and refuses to continue with this behavior. He does not take any of the cubes out of the cup.

7. He enjoys being rotated and laughs vigorously. He has minimal responses to being tipped to one side or the other, or tipped forward. He seems to enjoy play by the examiner with vigorous physical movements. When the examiner holds him in his lap in a somewhat uncomfortable position, his protest is never very strong, but at a later time when he is being held seated upright, he does protest vigorously but only by fussing. When he is held, he gradually calms. He is placed prone again to replace his clothing. He again fusses, just crying as though he were tired. He did not sleep on his way to the medical center today, and so his mother feels that he is somewhat tired.

His parents feel that there are a number of things he has done which demonstrate his alertness. When he was about 15 months old and they moved, he seemed to be quite concerned and cry when he noticed the furniture was moved. His mother feels that he has definite refusals to do things in his play, and he seems to demonstrate some today. He has tantrums when he is upset, although they are quite mild if today is any indication. His parents report that he picks up peas with his fingertips when he is feeding himself. He responds to various songs and nursery rhymes with appropriate physical behavior or showing his enjoyment or displeasure by laughing or by pushing the book away. His mother feels that he knows his own name, but there is no real evidence of that here today. He makes a definite release of the toys.

His parents have always felt that he is quite an alert and attentive child and for this reason have not felt that he is really retarded, although they were encouraged to think so. In discussing this with them briefly, I suggested that some of the things he did today were similar to those of a child of about one year in some ways. I would like to see him again very shortly to see if today is typical of his behavior. His parents were not sure that his behavior today was typical, although they did say that it was not very atypical. He will be admitted 1/25/65, and I will see him then.

Summary:

On the basis of John's performance today, he might be given the following scores as a reflection of his best performance; scored by interpolation and generously rated:

Area	Age	Developmental Quotient
Gross motor	4 months	18
Fine motor	9 months	41
Adaptive	13 months	59
Language	6 months	27
Personal-social	12 months	55

The adaptive performance score is a reflection of the cube and cup behavior; his involvement in the test was such that no score could be given in a standard way.

*

Pussycat, pussycat, where have you been?
To Medical School to visit the queen.
Pussycat, pussycat, what did you there?
I was frightened by a little thought under her chair.

Little John must go back to the hospital for a pneumoencephalogram—a bubble of air is inserted into the fluid surrounding the brain and tracked by X ray as the head is
tipped and tilted. This could reveal a "gross" abnormality
in brain structure, which would indicate a limit on his development and thus assist prognosis. Yet even if no such abnormality showed up, we would not be entitled to assume all is
normal. Nor can anything be done about it, whatever it shows.
The epicanthus folds, shaped like) (, at the inner corners of
his eyes, the sunken chest, the largish earlobes are all anomalous. Plus, mainly, "He hasn't made as much progress as we
would like him to by now."

Saturday,
January 9

At lunch I ran out to Lookout Rock, thinking about the
poor little fellow. Emily was reading of India, where "even
the imbecile brother must be provided with a wife and
home." And last night she said, "I feel I was so wicked to
have him." Stunned me.

She took a nap, then Ted and Christie turned up providen-
tially, as so often since they befriended us after the first
baby died. Little John did well in his posture jacket for
nearly an hour, we took a slow walk up the road, and the
afternoon passed.

Little John cried for an hour this morning before lunch
and for half an hour on going to bed. Is he "spoiled"? For
him, *demanding* is good.

Yesterday he "did not see" the little red candy placed

before him. Today Emily put one on his tray, and he reached for it at once.

Sunday, January 10

There is the question of adopting. Right now we feel not the faintest interest in children per se.

He squints his eyes, as if they suddenly smarted.

Monday, January 11

The *bite* is: The gnaw of day to day, the sameness of each, the absence of progress and change. Which makes us feel any change would be good. Especially there are these long times of yelling—hopeless moaning cries, screams, and squalls—when he is tired and has wakened, or needs to go to bed and doesn't want to.

Tuesday, January 12

Bad night with John James again, Emily up three times, I once. At school, in the washroom mirror, noticed circles under my eyes.

At home, found Emily and John very cheery. When he is "himself," like this, you can stand it. When not, you feel the grief.

Wednesday, January 13

Penelope has hemorrhaged. "This is a recurrence." She must decide between going to the City of Hope, a free hospital for cancer patients where she would have intravenous chemical treatments, and staying here without such treatments.

Did she *know* this was coming, in England, where she could also have had free medical care, and return deliberately with the knowledge? Or not knowing it, did she return with false hopes? Or more likely, for people know these things beneath their conscious knowledge, knowing it, and wishing to return here—in part, to return to *us?*

January 16-17, the weekend

—in which, beginning at the university library on Saturday morning, where we checked out a lot of books on mental

55   The Life of a Special Child

retardation, we accustomed ourselves to the implications of the fact that Little John clearly is such a case. Very bitter to acknowledge, and Sunday night our controls lifted as we thought of what the poor boy must face. Yet in spite of our distress it is important that Little John's life be as calm and good and happy as we can make it.

Planted five fruit trees along the front bank, giving order and shape to that empty slope.

Monday, January 18

Emily phoned Penelope, who has had to swallow the bad news straight: she must go to the City of Hope for treatments "to prolong life" and nothing further.

Tuesday, January 19

Put Little John down early with a cold, his first in a long year. Called a friend to ask about local pediatricians—we have now completely abandoned Dr. Eldridge. "There are really only two men for helping children with difficulties, and one is retiring soon. Call Dr. Hugh Riordan."

*

Before noon, I was getting ready to leave for class when Emily called me desperately, "John, come." I rushed into Little John's room to find him on his back, a large puddle of vomit on the sheet, his eyes open and not seeing. His body twitched symmetrically—feet and legs, fingers and arms, even cheeks and eyebrows—and his voice box was emitting soft, regular grunts or groans. I picked him up while Emily phoned Dr. Riordan, reaching his partner Dr. Shelton, and we drove fast into town. A hard, dry-handed, electric terror. Shelton gave him a sedative, but not until 12:30, after more than forty minutes, did the jerking stop. Something "other" was in control, the person himself no longer there. We stand outside a wall, looking into a room we cannot enter. From the clinic we took him straight to the hospital.

*

I had to wait for him at the X ray room. They wheeled him through on the gurney, pale, eyes closed, but his shock of silky fair hair outlining the delicate face. People around me gasped, "Oh, what a beautiful child, what's wrong with him?"

"We don't know."

"Oh, I do hope he gets better!" To them all he was a perfect, normal child.

Confusion among the doctors—all Little John's records are at the medical school. Dr. Shelton has never seen him before. Everything seems clouded. There's been a weight of unknowing ever since we were at the medical school ten days ago. Now I don't know what to think or feel or expect. I guess I expect the worst.

*

Home, we can relax, or at least sit and rest. Though after a little, how empty the house seems and how useless the free time.

Wednesday, January 20 When we got to the hospital this morning, late, he was awake and cooler but not conscious of our presence. He was hearing noises and disturbed by them—crib sides sliding up and down, babies yelling—but his cries were peculiar, and he didn't smile at all for the half-hour I was there. Emily stayed while I went off to give my classes.

We are frightened that the seizure might have injured the brain. And why did it begin? We prepare ourselves for the

57   The Life of a Special Child

absolute, and can imagine this as some dreadful and final thing, the end of whatever has been dragging him down. It would be much worse for it not to be final, yet to deprive him of even the little development he has achieved.

The department chairman called me to his office to ask if Emily would like to teach two sections of freshman English this spring, with a reader to help her. I blundered out something about Little John, and he said, almost gasping, "Oh no, John," his eyes wet.

At three the secretary opened the door of my classroom—a shock, as I had felt secure in there. Emily wanted me to come to the hospital right away, "though it's not an emergency." When I got there, Little John was sleeping, so we went for a long walk. She had called me because she had been deeply distressed by the doctor lecturing her about John in terms of "a hopeless case"— meaning not this seizure but the long-term view. Suddenly I realized, seeing him reduced to zero, how much we do have in him as he usually is—cheery, aware. How much there is, even in that, to lose, as we saw when his open eyes stared around at nothing.

When he woke at four, he looked more alert than at noon. But noises still irritated him, and he was crying when Dr. Shelton appeared, an hour later. Shelton thinks the cause of the seizure may be a defect in the central nervous system—the temperature controls go out of adjustment, and a high fever then leads to convulsion. Disturbing in that it suggests this could happen again. The idea exists in our minds that he may have developed as far as he ever will.

*

Dr. Shelton wanted to send him home today. I feel he's their responsibility—if he's this sick, he should be in the hospital. We are too frightened to have him at home yet. It is hard not to think, "If he were to die, it would be easier." He is crying with a strange high-pitched cry—"cerebral," they call it.

Since I didn't go into hysterics when he told me John James was a "hopeless" case, Shelton tried to enlist *my* sympathy for *his* problems. He complained that parents are often so angry when he tells them their baby is abnormal. For God's sake can't he see beyond *his* feelings to theirs?

The next day we brought Little John home. We too were hopeless, exhausted by anxiety and despair. We were receiving our new status passively, as even those moderate hopes we had been schooling ourselves to accept—that he would be more or less severely retarded and crippled—were now being terminated.

What the young doctor did not know to tell us was that the "hopelessness" of the case was not what mattered. It was not the statistical limits of his condition, as marked by DQ or IQ scores, that would define our child, any more than he was to be defined by the loss of our earlier hopes for him. Noticing the small changes in his skills, we would come to an understanding and acceptance of his limitations, and eventually we could almost say we welcomed them, as we learned to see the unique beauty that illumined them.

The emergency had caught us without a local pediatrician familiar with Little John's case, and it was clear that Shelton, whom we had reached by the accident of his partner being off duty, was not a man to lean on. But how were we to transfer Little John from his hands to those of one we thought would be better? It came about quite simply the next day. We phoned for advice about the vomiting that was still continuing; this time it was Shelton who was out of town, and Dr. Riordan who took the call. Somehow he had already seen Little John in the hospital, and from the way he talked he seemed to have grasped the situation more thoroughly than Shelton. His advice was brief but decisive, whereas Shelton, deferring to our apparent knowledge of Little John's condition, had remained indefinite. When we made a second call later the same day, Dr. Riordan sensed our need and threw us the lifeline we had been too timid to ask for: he offered to take over Little John's care, and we accepted eagerly.

Thursday, January 21

Helped Penelope move to a new apartment, which her mother doesn't like. Dark, under stairways. Small crowded rooms. "Well, it's a place to hang our hats."

On to the hospital, picking up Little John. Very weak, but he seemed pleased to be in my arms, and relaxed in the car. After sleeping all afternoon, he drank some milk but threw it up. Drank more milk later and held it down.

Mani phoned midafternoon: "Are you discouraged? Don't be discouraged, whatever happens." But she has been feeling it terribly, I could tell from her voice—her speech slower and more vibrant, from sorrow.

Quite possibly the sulfa medicine is causing the vomiting. It is being given to stop a hypothetical infection no one believes in. Dr. Riordan tonight said to take him off it. He is looking very thin and weak and has held down hardly any food today or yesterday. How long ago it seems since he sat in his highchair and banged the tray with his fists.

Friday, January 22

Emily up to him every half-hour or hour until 2:00 A.M.; then he slept until 5:00. This morning he is drinking more and has not vomited; even ate a little cereal.

Penelope's mother phones. Penelope hemorrhaged again this morning, after the bleeding had stopped for a couple of days. Is in bed resting.

Little John's temperature up again. At 2:00 P.M. we took him to Dr. Riordan for a shot of penicillin. Our first visit with him. He began, "You know that your child has a serious problem—" but we shied away, not wanting any more lectures. He gave an anticonvulsant; it seems that "these children" have convulsions easily.

Drove Penelope and her mother home from the General Hospital, where they had been inquiring about the cost of care. Both were very upset by the facilities there—no privacy. Penelope's mother whispered to me, "It's not good, John. He says there's no hope at all. A matter of weeks." I stayed with them an hour, had a drink sitting on the bed, Penny looking pale but cheery. When her mother said the doctor had told them, "As far as doctor's fees go, you don't need to worry about me," she remarked, "When I get my job, he'll be the first to be paid." Is it that she doesn't know, or knows but won't admit it? Or that as long as you are alive, you must talk in terms of living? On the phone to Emily, talking about her interview with the social worker, she spoke otherwise: "They would take Mother's last dime afterward to pay for my care. They made me feel like a pauper."

**Saturday,
January 23**

Perhaps the cruelest fear for us is that we may not be *able* to keep him at home. We are willing to do quite a hell of a lot to keep him with us.

Running through my mind has been the poem I have taught so often, Ben Jonson's "On My First Son," especially the last two lines, profound and puzzling:

*Farewell, thou child of my right hand, and joy;
My sin was too much hope of thee, loved boy:
Seven years thou wert lent to me, and I thee pay,
Exacted by thy fate, on the just day.
O could I lose all father now! for why
Will man lament the state he should envy,
To have so soon 'scaped world's and flesh's rage,
And, if no other misery, yet age?
Rest in soft peace, and asked, say, "Here doth lie
Ben Jonson his best piece of poetry."
For whose sake henceforth all his vows be such
As what he loves may never like too much.*

Sunday, January 24   (Writing by candle and firelight, the winds having blown a power line down)

This morning we took Little John to Dr. Riordan for more penicillin, before going to the medical school again tomorrow. After the shot he looked at us. "You know that your child has a very serious problem." Oh yes, we nodded. Again we didn't want to be hit on the head with it. But he looked at us hard and kept on. "It takes you several months to get used to the idea," he told us. Then, "This sort of thing makes you either weaker or stronger, and it clearly hasn't made you weaker. It's either a wedge or a bridge between you." As for the question of institutional care, he declared flatly, "Nobody can look after a child like this as well as the mother."

And then he took an unexpected direction. "It makes you examine a lot of things in your life. Your religion." (He was dressed in a suit as if he had come straight from church.) "There are three parts to a person—the physical, the emotional, and the spiritual. These children are the same as any others in spirit and personality."

And finally, quite astoundingly: "A child like this is a sacrament."

"A child like this is a sacrament!" Having an abnormal child makes one feel one has failed, one is outcast, doomed somehow to be not normal oneself. Vistas open out of pain and separation and ugliness. But a sacrament is a partaking of the holy, the truth, the center. Whatever one wants to think of God, even if only to dismiss him, the notion of the sacramental remains, a metaphor with many-layered meanings. To place it in the being of a helpless child—"a hopeless case"—is to offer an entirely different covenant with existence. We saw our life and our child in a new light, not as a source of darkness and misery, but as in some way closer to truth and spirit. We felt, at once and whenever we recalled it in the future, like climbers who unload their packs in the thin air of the peak, released and

almost floating, weightless. Suddenly there was order out of chaos. We could never be as hopeless or despairing again. This doctor, who had the courage, seeing our stricken faces, to speak out to us, had given us back our child to love.

On our way home we stopped to see Penelope, still feeling somehow transfigured, moving on a different plane. Our faces showed it, calmed, even shining, and for a while we could share our new privilege with her. The next morning we made the drive to the medical school for an ordeal of testing more rigorous and painful than any before.

Monday, January 25

All day with John James in the hospital, not the Infants Section this time, but with older children. Much pleasanter, children getting well and running about, and a kindly nurse admitted us. Little John didn't adjust badly and in the playroom this evening sat happy on my lap, the TV going with children's programs at which he laughed, and children all around us playing and talking. I sat in the rocking chair with him, pleased and also proud that he was not wholly out of place. When Dr. Meredith saw him, though, she was sure he was not as good at manipulating with his fingers as two weeks ago. Our worst dread is a rapid degeneration.

*

Fed him the avocado we had brought from our trees. Dr. Meredith and another specialist came to see him. "Quite a gourmet," they joked, and he smiled back. He sat propped on the bed, smiling a fragile, total smile. A lamb before the slaughter, I thought. He is himself, whatever they say he is.

*

"Is it necessary?" we have asked about this test, since it is painful and, very rarely, dangerous. We even wrote Dr.

63   The Life of a Special Child

Meredith to beg off this whole visit. But there is always the chance they will come across some nugget of information that may affect the future of his case. Or some other? And so we are going through with it.

Tuesday, January 26   To the hospital before breakfast to keep him calm until they took him off for the pneumoencephalogram. He was again happy, though not hungry. We held him in the tidy empty playroom, that unmatched early Southern California sun beaming through the slats, and we had to bear the thought that this was our last chance to look on him in complete innocent love. Later today we will know more, and what we will know can hardly give us comfort. Only that to know is to understand the true possibilities of our hope. We stand here, helpless, as they roll him away to their tests.

11:15 A.M.   He's not back.

1:15 P.M.   Up to see him. Under a plastic oxygen tent he looks very peaceful. He will have headaches and not feel so good, says Dr. Meredith. Will this not leave him worse than before? Isn't it a purely *academic* test?

Sharing his room are a boy, Brett, and a girl, Christine, just J. J.'s age, who understands only French, and cries "Maman" incessantly. Emily thinks her fever and bluish dark spots on her legs and arms and her pallor indicate leukemia. She is alone nearly always, as her mother works and her father will not visit her. Everybody is kind, but she has withdrawn from us all.

*

We talked with an English woman whose boy, aged four, has had convulsions and become increasingly retarded; he can no longer talk, yet he seemed normal a year ago. An

64   And Say What He Is

older child died of the same illness, and another at nine months of meningitis. The mother vents her bitterness on the doctors, the waiting around, the lack of concern for letting her know what they think. I wish she wouldn't but I can understand. We get better treatment because we ask for it, and we can ask for explanations and understand them when they are given. But doctors ought to be able to talk to people who haven't been to graduate school.

Emily vomited most of the night. Left her in the motel and came to the hospital midmorning, in time to get some juice into Little John, which the nurse had not been able to do. In the afternoon he was less happy, hotter, wouldn't drink. I sponged him steadily, slowly. About seven at night Dr. Meredith made her way to us; looked at him rather perfunctorily, raised the crib side, and nodded for me to follow.

She led me along to a small empty classroom, where she drew on a blackboard a diagram of the structure of the interior of the head as shown by a pneumoencephalogram. Nothing abnormal here. (So it *was* a needless test.) But the new electroencephalogram has revealed something not functioning properly in the right anterior portion of the brain. This, along with the clear changes for the worse in the last month, means that we may expect a progressive deterioration—a leveling off, a regression, or an up-and-down alternation of the two. And what is the life expectancy? "I don't know. If I had to stick my neck out, I would say months, perhaps years."

Like a guillotine, with a sudden, neat, final blow, complete.

I went back to Little John, and my tears were immediate, but brief, as Brett needed help to go to the bathroom. When I left, John and Christine were both lying face down, their hair identically blond, identically fated. I bought some cognac and drove to the motel not knowing how to

65   The Life of a Special Child

say what I had to say to Emily. I couldn't speak. Wept, and the words came later. We spoke of our future and John's until at last we could sleep.

Thursday, January 28

We slept moderately well until six. In my mind were two of Ben Jonson's lines,

*In small proportions we just beauties see
And in short measures life may perfect be.*

This morning we met Dr. Meredith by surprise in the hall. She seemed somewhat perturbed—her hand shaking a little and eyes perhaps again wet. We may have helped *her* a bit, because we accept. Because a tree has begun to grow in us whose fruit is the understanding of all this?

To buy Emily the most expensive bright red woolen knit suit we have ever bought is not a frivolous action.

*

We saw the developmental examiner again today. He is an idealist, a sensitive young man; he likes working with children because there *is* promise. The cruelest thing, he said, is to see a child cut off and the promise destroyed.

When he spoke to us about adopting, though, I said our luck with children hadn't been too good. He drew back, disturbed by my bitterness. And I felt mad. These doctors ought to be willing to let people express some of their anguish without getting embarrassed or cross. That's part of their job. And it is the only time I have done it, God knows. Dr. Meredith's eyes met ours, and hers were filled with tears. That's sharing it.

Friday, January 29

Quiet conversation in the alcove, with Dr. Meredith answering all our prepared questions—drugs, food, future. End?

Variable. More convulsions? Sedatives daily to prevent them. The nervous system is going downhill, but there may be a series of ups and downs. He may seem to do well for a while. The mechanism that's defective doesn't go on very long. It is a degenerative process, not atrophy. She wished us good luck, told us of a doctor friend of hers with a retarded child, who adopted a little girl so bright she's practically off the scale.

We left about twilight. John was happy to be in his portable crib in the car, well aware of the difference of place. Went to bed early.

Mani on the phone this afternoon offered to pay the difference between our insurance coverage and the hospital costs.

In the evening, Little John played on the floor, very like himself. Groaned at the whistling locomotive Ted and Christie gave him, raised his head and arched his back, turned over. It made us happy; yet the thought of his degenerating is harder when he is lively and happy than when he was droopy and not laughing in the hospital.

I sat him in my lap at the head of the dining table. I could see the side and back of his head reflected in the window—hair still sticking up in straws from electroencephalogram grease, head hanging. Then in the night beyond the glass, two headlights appeared on Oakcrest Ridge, heading this way, downhill. They flickered as thin-leaved branches interrupted their light. Then they went black—where there had been a course traced by them through the blackness, there was suddenly none. And then they came bright again for a little, flickered, then went out. This is an image, I thought, of him; not symbol or allegory, but image, a direct visual experience. The lights were now hidden, I presumed, beneath the shoulder of the near hill. Then for another

67 The Life of a Special Child

unexpected instant they reappeared near the bottom, as bright as at the top, before they were finally extinguished.

Sunday, January 31

Note: The body has only a few finely movable parts—the hands and fingers, the jaw and mouth, the eyes. The other moving parts are comparatively gross. Thus those few fine parts must be of special moment; and in his case they all show regression: the eyes crossing and wavering, the jaw hanging more open and the tongue sometimes protruding, the wrists weaker and the fingers not grasping and holding as they did, the arm shaking if he reaches for something. These are among the "clinical" signs against which the physiological tests are made as confirmations. He is a sick little boy after all, Emily says. *Faint angel.*

Wednesday, February 3

To Dr. Riordan this afternoon, Little John crying and arching the whole time. Dr. Riordan repeating some of what he said before, and not paying attention to Dr. Meredith's prognosis. He brushed aside what we said about John fading and getting worse: "He will get easier to look after as time goes on." We felt incredulous and a bit annoyed; it seemed like not facing facts. I suppose his idea is that however long John's time may be, we have to live with him—to make the best life we can for all of us.

*

A call from Penelope's mother, here for the weekend from the City of Hope. Penny is offered—gratis—incredible surgery as a "last hope;" not much of her would be left. It seems insane to us, but she sees it as deliberately committing suicide to refuse—and is consulting a priest on this point. If this is the price of free medical care—a guinea pig operation—it is too high.

During this time the patterns of our lives also were changing significantly. After Little John's convulsion we had had to forgo all our training of him; not progress but stasis was now our best hope. For the first time, in the bitter despair that followed his stay in hospital, we were willing to give up a major portion of his care to someone else—to ask for help. Luckily, through friends at the school where Emily had taught after the loss of our first baby, we found a good person, Frannie, the mother of one of the teachers there, who had looked after a child with leukemia. Freed for five mornings a week, Emily returned eagerly to teaching at the university for the spring term.

February 10   It is strange to have dropped entirely all our pushing of Little John toward achievement and development. Yet also a great relief. We have been pushing him to learn things he couldn't, uphill against a stream that was running fast and deep downhill. And he was feeling the strain. I see now why he was so cross last month. Perhaps the convulsion was the culmination of that strain, some inner refusal not recognizable in medical terms. Now our hope is merely to keep him happy. He *was* happy in learning new skills for many of those months, delighted in each new achievement, but the current has become too strong lately, and for us it is a relief to stop and float down with it. He is happy with what he can do now, but not with the things that have already become too hard.

March 1   Came home from my new classes anxious about Frannie's leaving to have a major operation. We are already so dependent on her help. However, she brought a friend of hers today, named Rosalie, who can take over part-time until I find someone permanent. As I walked in, there was Little John on Rosalie's shoulder, skillfully held, and as she swung around to me, I saw his happy smile—he won't smile unless he likes the person holding him—and then Rosalie

69   The Life of a Special Child

gave a lovely smile too. I felt, it's all right, it will be all right.

March 4 This place is growing on us. I love it, the chaparral full of flowers, the garden already calling me to weed and plant it. When Little John is napping in the afternoon, I stroll down the driveway and feel a chill on my skin under the warm sun. The weather has been so clear. Last summer when we were buying the place, Penelope said, "What a lovely ocean view." I had scarcely noticed it under the fog and said, "Oh, it is the mountains we love." But she was right. The sky and air and sea all shimmer on these clear crisp days. This niche below the mountains heals us.

March 6-7 Drove over to visit Penelope at the City of Hope. Her mother had warned us not to be shocked at her appearance. It was not really so shocking except that when we arrived she was lying very low in the bed and quiet, her face more hollow-cheeked and without animation. But she roused herself and joked about flirting with her doctor from home, who had been over to see her.

Her doctor there, a young woman, told us the prospect is for two to four *weeks*, not months. We arranged to come back in three days and drive Penny back to the local community hospital—*not* the General—"so she can die among friends."

Does Penelope's refusal to *accept* the finality of this thing stem, not from being afraid to, but from courage, a fighting spirit unwilling to give up? Between us it is unspoken, but seems known.

Wednesday, March 10 The trip went better than we expected. Penelope's face was the face of Christ in Van Meegren's *The Supper at Emmaus*, a light shining out and through, amid deep shadows.

*

John had improvised an ambulance bed in the back of the station wagon, and it was comfortable once she had struggled onto it. When we came to the coast, sharp and brilliant in the afternoon sun, I roused her to look. I felt she *should* see it, for the last time, while she could.

When we got to Emergency, we found there was no bed for her upstairs. How could they do this! The doctor had promised there would be a place for her. And the aides were so incompetent, doing nothing to lift or help her. Such rage I felt, since we had tried so hard to make it all go smoothly. "She's dying!" I wanted to shout at them.

Thursday, March 11

A terrible shock to see Penelope this morning. Overnight her face had become a death mask, her eyelids half open although she was asleep.

Tonight I sat with her to give her mother a rest, while John was driving to the airport to meet her sister, flying from Paris. I felt I must try to hold Penny here, keep her alive, until her sister arrived. Mostly she lay quiet, not asleep but not really conscious. But she roused and smiled with such joy when her sister came in after midnight; it transfigured her face. Her spirit shines through it. Otherwise she's like a corpse, but that smile overcomes it, and then she—*she*—is beautiful.

Friday, March 12

Little John's second birthday, which we ignore. His fate is a secret we keep from Penelope and her mother. When I came back from school this morning, Penelope was more corpselike than last night. We could not tell what she wanted—unpredictably she raised herself and sat upright in bed, saying crossly, "Why can't I get up?" and then lay back. But she turned her smile toward me when I spoke

71 The Life of a Special Child

and gave her some orange-scented flowers to smell. She understood and put them to her nose. As I left, she raised her hand and waved good-bye. "She is still there!" I said to myself as I drove away home, astonished.

*

I went in this afternoon, John having felt from his morning visit that we must talk to her, and be there, until she is really gone. She *is* there when we call her. She rouses and then she lives rather than dies. I was too late. Yet at first I could not tell in the quiet room if she was alive or not, so close to death had she looked before.

I joined her mother in the "Family Room," where we waited for the undertaker before going to get her things. When he came, he was fawning and unctuous and by some gross error kept referring to Penelope as "him." I had to control the impulse to laugh hysterically. This week has been all hers. Always a feeling of being close to an abyss ourselves.

*

Her look is with us—Emily says *in* us. Lying in bed last night, she felt Penelope's look to be taking over hers. It is long enough for us to have seen and understood. Dear God, I thought, your message is coming through.

For a while we were numb from the intensity and strain of the past weeks. We had wondered, often, if Penelope's catastrophe, coming so close upon our own, would push us past some breaking point. We began to turn our main attention again to Little John's care, which was becoming rapidly more specialized; his balance seemed so delicate that even the slightest jarring of his routine, we believed, might be fatal. We were sure the end would come soon—"months," Dr. Meredith had predicted, "*per-haps* years." Under this sentence new strains began to show, despite the increasing skill of Rosalie's assistance. Outside disappointments—the grandfather's flat refusal to visit us from New Zealand, the university's invoking of the nepotism rule to prevent Emily from teaching in the fall—bulked large and stunned us. And in the aftermath of Penelope's death we feared for Little John's life more anxiously than ever. A few days away alone, arranged with difficulty, helped but little.

Sunday,
April 18

IN THE TIMBER

*We leave town, our one
boy, blue-eyed, blond
as a Prince of Norway, but
impeded beyond hope
of ever hastening; and we
hasten to the near distance,
climbing by edge of gulch,
rapid, and fall, to timber
hiking up a double-peaked
ridge, whose small, high
valley between tells us
the San Andreas Fault
runs through, under our feet.*

*We let go our touch to descend
the steep hillside footing
to a small stream of live water
wavering over glittering sand
and seaweed-dark moss, where we sit
like some old married couple
in an Impressionist painting
sur l'herbe, watching the water.*

Drunk on pure mindlessness,

73 The Life of a Special Child

> *half sexual heat, half sweat,*
> *we sat apart on the one rock.*
> *All our family left at home,*
> *we counted nothing, we saw*
> *three flowers, two the same one;*
> *and we watched our selves there drift*
> *as if we were swimming on the high*
> *air swells among the pine tops,*
> *uncertain even of their kinds.*

April 19 When Little John is happy, we all are ecstatic, but when he cries or is fretful, we are cast down. There's his dying in those cries. We swing so, every day. We watch the little changes, and we even seek them out so we won't be caught napping, yet each one cuts through us. Then he laughs at a toy, starts giggling, and we feel euphoric.

April 21 [From a letter to a friend from graduate school]

I battled the administration personally, rank by rank up to the vice-chancellor, trying to get the nepotism rule waived. All I achieved was a new understanding of bureaucracy—each level passes the buck to the next. As a bribe, now, they have given me a contract, with a raise, to teach remedial writing. I am humiliated, because it is a Mickey Mouse department, run with outmoded methods by a foolish and arbitrary man. But beggars, it seems, can't be choosers. Before, my teaching meant much more than the money; it affirmed another self for me than the nurse-mother.

Saturday, April 24 The whole week has been *hot,* with wild winds every night —like being in the bottom of a gully with flood water crashing over, rolling stones, blocking, then rushing free in a great large current. Little John couldn't get to sleep because of it Thursday night.

Today we took him to the beach. He first was terrified by the waves, then in a short while became delighted and kicked and splashed with his feet. His walking movements are getting more awkward, one foot stepping on the other at the end of each little series of kicking steps. It is possible now to see the leftward-leaning direction of his nervous system degeneration: the left arm twists more than the right, the spine seems to curve that way, and the left foot and leg aren't as skillful as the right. He is just as happy as ever, though, and that surely is what must matter most.

The wind is terrible tonight. Each time it has been like a hideous messenger whose word is nothing.

What kept us going from day to day and helped to steady the whole course of our lives was our helper Rosalie. Unmarried, the fourth child of an upper-class New England family that had moved to California when she was a girl, she had begun her adult life by nursing her invalid father for six years. After ten years as a dental technician in another city she had been called home to nurse her mother through a long illness. Now with the death of her mother she was adrift and happy to become a member of a family again. She continued her friend Frannie's routines with Little John but soon developed new ones of her own, and her patient good humor in tending him—bathing, walking him in his stroller up the steep, hot road, persuading him to eat, to laugh, to play—became essential to the quiet and the freedom of the household. We could never have helped Penelope if Rosalie had not kept everything going at home, nor could we both have continued teaching. We did not like the thought that she would be with us only temporarily.

May 4   To Dr. Riordan today, who spoke of the reality we must face with Little John and said he thought he *could* detect some signs of deterioration since our last visit a few weeks ago. Warned us of the strains *we* are under, which we were aware of in a sort of mutual bickering over the weekend.

75   The Life of a Special Child

"You've got a very, very bad situation here—I don't know
of any worse situation that you could have."

THE GRAPHS
(In time of a Gemini space flight)

1

Clean-scrubbed, our two-year-old son
Laughs from his belly behind his crib's slats,
Arching his back and scrambling his legs down—

The most vigorous of all his acts. Growing dark,
The day glides downward like a huge plane,
The ridge mass a solid variable mark

Descending the crossbars of the patio trellis
According to a steep formula, sharp
As that of grief marring the chart of hopes

We had sketched hesitantly across
In a smooth wash of clear possibles,
Seeking any charm against loss.

2

The sky behind the peaks is all dim.
In the next room, by the night-light,
A cockerel, fighting sleep, I hear him

Now turned face upward, gentling
The red plastic ring of his crib gym
With fingers that can only faintly cling.

I am bedded too, over a muscle spasm
And a burned heart. Blanking,
The light has abandoned the mountains:

Casting out, the eyes are thrown back
Upon themselves and the room: windows

Turn mirrors, and the graph sinks black.

3

My wife cut me a rose today
As she does for the sick. It drinks
From her water glass. As always

We seek these beauties that will cease,
And splash down, heavy with the full weight
Of ourselves, into the thickening mother sea

Where, should a raft inflate for us,
It floats compassless. If we may
Raise this golden bud to our noses,

May we not also hope? No. Hope
Is not instrumental as a rose,
But thorny, and hid blood-deep.

June 21 [From a letter to the grandfather]

A few days ago Dr. Riordan said I should have more help with Little John, so I asked Rosalie if she would consider staying all day. It turned out that she wanted to very much and in fact couldn't afford to work part-time any longer.

John leaves in one week to do some research at a library too far to travel to every day. He will be there until the end of July on a special summer fellowship—something of an honor—staying all week with friends and coming home for weekends. We are afraid that Little John may be difficult without his father here, and I don't look forward to the evenings by myself, I must say. Little John is not content unless one of us is there doing things for him most of the time. He can't pick up his toys very easily, and if he drops one, he gets upset, so that you can't even get the dishes done without many interruptions. Also, someone else has to hold him now while I feed him. I had a tremendous struggle getting him to eat when John's back was hurt.

If it is too hard, John will just have to give up the scholarship, but we hope not, as it is a fine chance for him to get some solid work done at a specialized library, and we need the extra money badly. For one thing, it will help pay for Rosalie's longer days.

July 15

I am thrown back on myself these days, and I don't like it. I need John here to temper Little John's crying spells, to call on when it gets too much for me. And I enjoy Little John more when John is here too. I hate the nights, nervous even though I know it's foolish. I wish Rosalie could stay, but she needs some time by herself.

John and I have been quarreling each weekend and finally reached a terrible state. Dying for him to come home, happy when he arrives, then, perhaps resentful of his freedom, I start something. But each time, when we try to discover *what* we are quarreling about and can't find any definable cause, we realize it is our grief for Little John, our sense of our lives not going forward but stopped, self-devouring. We stand over him, fearful of every change because it will cut down his future. During one quarrel I found myself thinking: If only I could fall in love with someone else and run away and start all over. Not so much a formulated thought as a gut longing. As if I could leave either John.

**Monday,
July 19**

Singularly sweet we were to each other all weekend. I arrived home on Friday, saying I don't know how much longer I can stand this separation, and I'll do anything you want me to all weekend. And I did. And in ten days I'll be home for good.

August 10

[From a letter to the grandfather]

We are having real summer weather, and it is hard on

78   And Say What He Is

Little John when the air is so stifling because his "thermo-
stat" doesn't work properly and he doesn't sweat. But it is
cool at the beach, and he loves the water. We are going to
spend the last week of August at the beach, near Mani, in
a kitchen apartment, with Rosalie along so we will be able
to be free sometimes.

As the summer has gone by, it has become clearer and
clearer that we need a normal child to help us not to con-
centrate too much on Little John and not to grieve too
much. We have tried to distract ourselves with our jobs and
a busier social life, but the gap between our longing for a
normal family and its absence has grown more and more
painful. We both love children so much, and now that our
feelings have been aroused in caring for Little John, we
need a child. We dare not try to have another baby—all the
doctors say the risk is too great. And so we are dealing with
the people in the adoption agency here. We like them, and
they seem intelligent and humane in their concern for both
the children they get and the parents they deal with.

*

In a book on adoption, an eleven-year-old adopted boy
says: "The child who is born into his family is like a board
that's nailed down from the start. But the adopted child,
him the parents have to nail down, otherwise he is like a
loose board in mid-air."

Together again, the boy
gold on the golden couch, happy
under the soft rigors of Handel—
another of the musics he likes;
you in the kitchen in late sunlight,
while I stand to write this

79 The Life of a Special Child

on the mantelpiece, my eyes smarting,
partly with smog, partly excess of joy.

August 26.
The Beach.

[From a letter to the grandfather]

We have been doing things we can never do at home. Tonight, John and Rosalie walked to the movies, after she had taken the helm while we took a stroll on the esplanade—it was wonderful to listen to the waves on the rocks, the white swirls of foam occasionally visible in the darkness. We have even been able to browse in a bookstore at night! Rosalie is enjoying it, too. It's a good friendship among the four of us.

Little John has so much pleasure in what he can do and is as happy as he can be. He kicks ecstatically on the mat, arms out ahead of him, head down with the effort, and throwing his legs back up high in the air. And he loves the ocean. We go to a small bay where there is a clear bubbly surf and large grains of very clean sand. He would stay in forever, and poor big John is all sunburned from holding him in the jumper jacket so he can dangle and kick his feet in the waves.

His meal routine is comic. We wonder what the people below us must think. At seven, at noon, and at five, precisely, the same recording of Baroque trumpet concertos blasts out brilliantly until he has eaten his soft mashed food, and then off! It's such a gay triumphal sound. Without it he won't eat, and even with it we have to talk fast sometimes.

August 28

Mani met us on the beach and sat with us. She urged that, no matter what the doctors say, we should keep on fighting. "Never give up hope," by which she means hope that he will be "all right." "Don't give in. His intelligence is so superior that his mental retardation simply means . . ."

that he comes level with ordinary children? I shook my head. I felt such pain that she would keep these false hopes, which will only hurt her the more.

What we are trying to do is face the truth and survive it. Is it "giving in" to know that he may die at any time? It doesn't help to be urged not to be honest. We face the worst and still try to be happy. We *have* been happy in this week here—extravagantly happy.

At one point she suggested we could have intravenous feedings for him. I was appalled. More hospitals, pain, Little John tied in bed to a silver needle.

August 29   Talked to my brother about Mani having false hopes about Little John. "Yes, we can see you are looking after him quite well, but are you doing enough? I wouldn't stop until I'd taken him to every clinic in the country and found the answer." But there isn't any "answer." Mani is angry because we are not taking her advice, and we are accused of not considering *her* feelings. We had grown closer to her lately, and it hurts to have this support cut away.

*

We didn't get angry enough. Surely they could guess what a daily struggle it is to keep going when you are caring for a dying child.

August 31   Our last day of vacation, still feeling shaken by family dissension. We spent it mostly on the beach. A buffeting sea, exhilarating to swim in, and Little John ecstatic as he jumped his feet in the waves. He seems stronger, holds his head up longer, and looks around more. He is more aware than a few months ago and recognizes Rosalie with a welcoming smile.

SON ON THE FLOOR

Golden lad, eating lint in the
pile of the dirty carpet:
who would ever want to think
you will form part of it?
Only some pill-fed Presbyter
with a glower like gray guy-wires.

We gaze on you with different
eyes: you are the golden dawn,
a bud as purely consumed
as any in Eden,
an ideal son for Abraham,
flushed, unreluctant, to tie down.

Persevere: so as you do, you
chew, you will provoke the dust,
fall face down tasting it and
raise up. I cannot but
praise with my eyes, and if there is
a Jesus, teach him joy with yours!

September 1   When we got home, while I was setting up his crib again in
his room and Emily was getting his lunch ready, he, left on
our big bed bouncing happily, worked his way to the edge
of it and off, with a terrifying thump. Blood in his mouth.
"He's smashed his teeth!" I yelled. Emily hid her eyes.
"Oh no." It was only a cut lip, but he was intensely
distressed.

I walked him around on my shoulder for a long while,
soothing him, haunted by the image I could picture: his
limp body slipping and flopping free, his face striking the

hardwood floor, then the pause, then the cry. But he *did* cry. There's less danger of concussion since he did. Finally he ate a little lunch, slept well, and has shown no ill effects.

September 5   Killed a small rattlesnake today, which Emily discovered at her feet in the long weeds around the avocado trees. We might not have thought it had to be killed except that we leave Little John out on his mat in the patio by himself sometimes.

Walking this afternoon up our road to the grounds of the Zen Center pushing Little John in the stroller, I had what struck me as an Asian thought: "If John were not as he is, the universe would not be perfect." Emily amended *perfect* to *complete.* The Buddha said, "All compounded things are suffering"; this accepts every form of suffering as necessary, therefore "good" or at least not *evil.* This seems a more realistic view of the universe than the Christian, but it rejects happiness. The Christian view may be more *brave:* "It is a brave act of valor to contemn death; but where life is more terrible than death, it is then the truest valor to live." (Sir Thomas Browne, *Religio Medici*) There is Little John's *valor,* as there was Penelope's.

Very shortly we would be changing our lives again. Our adoption application seemed to be moving especially fast, and by the end of September we realized we had better be getting our household in order for a new baby. That fall we were also both teaching again, and without Rosalie we could not have hoped to add another child to the complicated family. In fact, the adoption agency recommended that we get more help, since Little John was demanding such close attention. By chance, Emily's aunt Stella in New Zealand had recently retired from a long career in nursing and offered to visit for two or three months to help us settle the baby in.

The baby would be two months old when it came to us—old enough to have been checked over thoroughly by a pediatrician, since we felt unable to take on another child with great physical or mental handicaps. Also we had asked for a girl, so that we would be less tempted to treat the baby as a replacement for Little John.

For what was already happening with him seemed to be what Dr. Meredith had predicted: a fairly rapid decline, though with alternating ups and downs. One day he would be full of vigor; a few days later he would seem deathly ill. It would be comforting to have a trained nurse in the house, along with the new baby.

September 9   Dr. Riordan says that Little John's total condition seems unchanged since May, and he is tougher—all that swimming and wave-kicking at the beach—so he could withstand a cold better now. We needn't feel so fearful of the baby giving him one. Certainly he is vigorous at the moment.

September 20   The sudden deathly pallor hit Little John just before breakfast. This hasn't happened for months, and it caught us completely by surprise. Dr. Riordan says it is the blood sugar suddenly dropping to a very low level, and we must force sugar or dextrose into him. We squirted two syringes of sugared fruit juice into the back of his mouth and then got him to eat a lot of toast with butter and brown sugar. He wouldn't eat his cereal. Rosalie persuaded him to drink some milk from his bottle, and soon he was himself. It is hard not to panic: the color simply drains from his face, and he looks ghastly.

September 21   Phoned by the adoption agency. Emily and I went into town together, to hear a description of the baby girl and her background. She sounds *just right.* Emily wept for the mother when we were told about her.

September 25   Aunt Stella at the airport—her voice surprisingly soft. Very pitying of Little John. What he needs is compassion—not pity but compassion.

September 28   Meeting the little girl who may become our Peggy. This is a very different experience from seeing your own newborn infant for the first time. There, emotions well up out of your body, like springs of water out of the ground, without thought. Here, they follow upon much careful thought: you plan and construct an aqueduct to carry the water to your desert, then gradually the land becomes fertile. When we came home a little somber, Stella helped lift our spirits with lighthearted, commonsense remarks: babies *are* babies; it's only as they grow with your care that you come to love them and know them. By comparison with Little John's beauty as a wee baby—or what I remember as his beauty— this little girl is not beautiful. But . . . it is because of what he is and can and cannot be that we are to have her.

Tonight we are quiet at home. Stella has thoughtfully gone off to bed. Quietly and calmly we hear the water begin to flow in a distant pipe, and the braces and supports shift slightly as the pipe begins to hold its weight.

September 29   Today we picked up Peggy from the agency. Both John and I held her in the office, and she seemed pleased with us and was very sweet in the car, turning her head around to look at John. There was a moment when she seemed to relax her scrutiny, and her gaze became contented. We feel a pure tenderness, a flooding of content. Rosalie, Stella, and Little John were out, and we were all alone with our new baby.

A bit hectic tonight. She was happy only when held, unsettled by the change of household.

*

Now there are no doubts, no questions, and she is smiling at us, looking around her new home, and already she seems to trust us. Suddenly we are four. What a difference! The whole pattern of relations suddenly changes. It is a new family. Little John is now a brother—a *big* brother! Tonight he seems aware of the difference, fussing a bit.

The moment we had feared, though, when the baby would cry for the first time in Little John's hearing, has come and gone. We all hushed, expecting him to wail. And he laughed! She must have sounded like a squeaky toy.

Saturday, September 30

Another very hot day. Took Little John to the beach twice, again. In the afternoon while I was swimming and Emily holding him, he suddenly went very limp. She waved me in, and I swam fast. Drove home quickly and revived him with sugar.

Sunday, October 1

Today he continued pale, and we feared the worst, as did Stella, who thought him close to a seizure. Dr. Riordan made a house call but did not think anything seriously the matter. "He's not *dying* on you. He won't suddenly go *out* like a light." But the little boy seems frailer, his head droops more often, and his color is always faint. And yet his temper is more cheery. He's a paradox.

We asked Dr. Riordan about places where Little John could go if he ever became too sick and helpless for us to take care of him. He got angry and repeated what he had said before, "The mother always looks after him best. He'll get easier to care for." We said that Dr. Meredith had suggested some day it might be better to put him into a good private home. "Any decent ones cost over three hundred dollars a month. Do you have that kind of money? Do you want me to put his name down for a state institution?" Of course we said no.

It was reassuring, one of our nightmares being that we might have to part with him because we could no longer care for him properly. At the same time, we sometimes feel the need of a place we could turn to if he really did get a great deal worse. The pediatrics textbook speaks of "increasing dementia," a phrase that terrifies us.

October 11 Peggy's solid little body and bright eyes watching everything promise so much. She seems to have accepted the change of home completely. There is a firm intentness about her that charms everyone. We all fight to hold her and care for her. Little John is becoming aware of her, staring at her sometimes in a very puzzled way. He also laughs at her and occasionally gives her a radiant smile.

October 13 We noticed Peggy today lifting her head up as high as a head would go from the prone position. Much earlier than Little John did it, and much higher.

Every morning now when Rosalie arrives, she dances Little John, smiling and laughing on her shoulder, to Beatles music. He no longer enjoys our classical records—any plaintive note from the strings, and off he goes in a wail. His beloved Baroque trumpet concertos are acceptable only until their slow movements. The Beatles give him happy sounds all the time. Stella, we think, would like to disapprove of the Beatles, on principle, but when she sees Little John's mirth, his wriggles of pleasure, his laughter at favorite passages, she just can't, and in fact she is growing to like them as the rest of us have!

November 8 Little John is angelic these days and seldom irritable. Since Peggy has come, he seems more settled. He *is* the older one, and despite his handicaps he is more mature, if only because more complicated. There is a beauty about him

87 The Life of a Special Child

now that transcends the strangeness in his eyes and the pallor. We have a sense of a mystery, a meaning here which only imperfection can make perfect and only the loss and absence of faculties can make whole. He is God's child. An uncommon joy, and it is made more complete by the presence of the little normal one. The contrast does not hurt us but merely *underlines*. I remember that in some ways he was more aware and more formed at this age than she is, though less strong and able. At this age his smile was fully developed, while hers is tentative. At times I have felt an intense grief that he could not get up and come to stand and watch her, but I never feel a real comparison between them. He is what he is.

November 20   [From a letter to a friend from graduate school]
It's quite a hectic life, being a working mother! Not much time to breathe the air, enjoy the slant of light, and barely enough to grade my papers, prepare for class, dress, make lunch for everybody, bolt mine, and dash off to campus. I like the students for the most part, though I don't like what I have to teach them. I *guess* the job is worth it.

December 1   Peggy wakes for a bottle at 3:00 A.M., as she does every night, and is hard to put down after. Little John wakes, cross and hungry, at six. I'm near tears when Rosalie arrives for the day, having had him fussing and whining for two hours. Perhaps there was some rational alternative—he must be tired, waking so early: put him back in bed for a while? But neither Emily nor I thought of it. The trouble is we become so tired—are so deeply, heavily exhausted—that we don't *think* of the rational alternatives. Debilitated.

December 3   I have resigned from my job in remedial English. When the director arbitrarily refused to schedule my two classes in consecutive hours, so that I could be away from home as little as possible, I got angry, he started blustering, and so I just hung up. Somehow we will manage to pay Rosalie without my salary. And while I have loved teaching, it has kept me away from Peggy.

December 8 Peggy is developing fast, yet I am always eager for more—the next step. Yesterday I lifted her by her hands, pulling her up from her infant seat several times and praising her. She became very excited. I wept. The long months of doing that with Little John, the encouragement and praise, all to no end.

December 10 Yesterday John and I had taken both kids for a walk in their strollers. At the corner of Hidden Canyon Road we met a young woman with a little girl in a stroller. She said hello, then asked if Little John was tired and, before we could answer, said, "What a beautiful little boy." As John began awkwardly to explain about his limpness, she said, "I have had a retarded child myself, I know." She let it all out with a rush, as we walked together up the road to her mother-in-law's house.

Her boy was two and a half when he died after chronic bronchitis, which twice turned into pneumonia. He was totally inert and helpless, able to cry when hungry but otherwise unaware. "Perhaps he knew the difference between light and dark. But you love them, you love them more because they are helpless, you want to protect them." Her voice was high, thin, and sad, almost wailing. "He was put in Pacific State Hospital two months before he died—the doctor said it was best. I was losing weight, he didn't even know the difference, he didn't recognize us. He had wonderful care. They fight to keep them alive, they give them everything. He was in an oxygen tent all the time.

89 The Life of a Special Child

"Oh, when the specialist first told me, it was heartbreaking. I closed into myself, I didn't even go out or see people, and it was always a strain to take him out in public. He held his head up very high when he was born, and that's bad, they shouldn't be able to do that.

"The day I went to Pacific State to see the place, it was terrible, I could hardly drive home. The bodies had shrunken from just lying there and never being used, just great big heads. They don't let you in the ward except once before you put your child in. But they do what they can. They do research. We donate what we can afford. That's our cause now."

The little girl she was pushing in the stroller had been born five months after the boy died. "And now we are afraid. Should we have another baby? We love her and she's perfect, but to have all that suffering again."

The grandmother came out from her house and met us. She spoke of Dennis, the dead grandson, and then of Little John. "Oh, but you should have hope. Look, he smiles at me. Dennis never did that." We said, "He used to be better than he is now."

My first quick thought was "It was merciful that Dennis died." Yet it was a genuine grief for her to lose the little creature she loved, as it will be for us, and we will angrily push aside those who give us glib comfort: "It's a mercy, the lifting of a great burden."

Coming back, John and I felt again a certain strange happiness, relieved through sharing our sorrow for the first time with another whose sorrow was similar but greater. And gradually a tremendous gratitude has risen in me. No longer do I feel I cannot endure Little John's touchiness, but rather I think of all he has given us, the happiness, the pure beauty of spirit unmixed with normal self-assertive drives. Last night I found myself looking at him and feeling so grateful that I have this little boy and that I have had the joy of a pregnancy issuing in the birth of a beautiful baby. Why carp about not being able to repeat it? And why ever dare to complain about what he is? "The universe would not be complete without him." He is *our* child, *our* mystery, our *own* sacrament.

1966

Little John on his table tonight, hitting the blue stuffed rabbit onto the floor with a clean, controlled swipe like a tennis serve. Since it is a blue rabbit he punches, we call the punch a "blue *rabbit punch*," meaning "a short chopping blow delivered to the base of the skull."

It is done with tantalizing skill and precision. We set the rabbit up for the punch, balancing it on the wobbly surface of the table pad. He pauses, like a boxer who taunts his opponent with a split-second warning, then chops it suddenly. As it disappears over the edge, we exclaim at his murderous brutality, and he giggles and snorts like a mad gamekeeper. We must promptly retrieve it—there's a string around its neck to pull it up swiftly—and set it up again, for this is an impatient puncher. Fortunately, though, it's a magic rabbit, and pops up ready for punching again as fresh as a bluebell. The magic is part of the game, and it's a game he always wins, until he's tired of it.

[From a letter to an aunt in England]

When he wakes from a deep sleep, his eyes have an odd transparence, and he often makes peculiar faces. But when he laughs, he is beautiful, and he *does* smile at us and recognize us, almost more than before.

These nights, while John prepares for his classes out in the study, I hold Little John stretched across my lap on the rocking chair, since he won't go to sleep yet and he won't lie in bed happy, and we rock together while I sing to him, for an hour. It is very peaceful, so I do not begrudge the time, and I am glad to enjoy him. I think we have come close to a real acceptance of our lot, not so often repining about what might have been. We have had a year with him like this now, and he seems just right as he is.

January 30   What a skill it has become, putting Little John to sleep. First you boost him onto your shoulder, resting his head on the thick folded diaper—if you forget it, he thinks it a great joke to take the soft skin between his strong little teeth and *bite*—hard enough, once, on his father to cause a blood blister! Then you start walking him up and down the darkened room, a long while, sometimes half an hour, until he stops raising his head, or giggling, or griping. All the time you are softly, rhythmically patting his back, listening for his breathing to slacken and ease. As he quiets, you slow your pace, being especially careful not to make a sound. Stand on the creaky board in the corner, and he's wide awake. Finally you can lower him carefully from your shoulder, changing hands to support his head and neck—if the shoulder cloth slips, it may fall on his face and wake him—and then, awkwardly bending and twisting, you lay him down on the mattress on his back. All silent and surreptitious, you slowly turn him onto one side, and prop him with a folded cloth so that he won't roll back. Perhaps he will heave a sigh, or startle—you hold your breath. Wait. Then when you're sure he's settled, creep away to the door, avoiding the creaky board again, out to the hall, pull the door softly closed—you've made it! And very likely you'll have it all to do again in the middle of the night, when you are all bleary and floppy from sleep, and barely able to exercise the skill and patience that even then are required.

February 4   Stella has left, and although she was a great help, she was not always at ease with us. We could never convince her not to pity Little John. She talked mournfully about him, while we would speak cheerfully. Once she said, "It would

93   The Life of a Special Child

have been much easier if he had been inert, so much less sorrow for you." This ignores the joy that Little John has brought. And besides, he *is,* he exists, and so the world has been changed by his existence.

Where existence is, there is God. Where love can be given, there is God. Where love *is* given, God *is.* What is good must not be rejected because it is mixed with pain or the threat of loss. We do have to live for the moment and not spoil the present or regret the past for fear of losing the joys now known.

<table>
<tr><td>Sunday,
February 6</td><td>*A Good Day!* Little John an angel, after several days of irritability, so I was easily able to look after both babies at once. Peggy had her juice bottle on the big bed while he played beside her. Then I popped her into his crib while I bathed him on his table. Then put him out on the mat in the back room while I bathed her next door. Put her to bed for a nap while he kicked and then had juice. Then he kicked happily for ages before taking a long nap until four. Later, he lifted his head ("way uppity-air") and turned it to smile at Peggy on the mat beside him, a big brother showing off. She smiled at him when he made his talking sounds. He seems to like her more and more, and she stares and stares and then, as today, sometimes smiles. In bed he likes to look up at Minna's zebra painting, black and white stripes on a bright yellow background, over the head of the crib. But when he kicks and lifts his head, he seems very frail—surely he is having more difficulty than just a few weeks ago.</td></tr>
<tr><td>February 20</td><td>Peggy watched shadows on the wall today. Six months old. So was it really anything amazing that Little John noticed them at thirteen months?</td></tr>
</table>

She jabbers now whenever we do, starts gabbling as soon

as there's any conversation. She pops her head up out of the buggy, two blue eyes just visible over the edge—"I was a spy in a baby buggy for the FBI."

FOR LITTLE JOHN APPROACHING THREE

What bird pursues its shadow
Down the rolled valleys of your brain
No specialist presumes to explain.

Those fields which lie all fallow
No plow's sharp tongue can ever turn,
Whatever seeds fall there must burn

In gay intensities of joy
Or chafe to the dark scrapings of sorrow.
No crop is looked for there tomorrow:

That yellow hill, soft banked,
Waves with bright weeds, not fat combed wheat.
A silver rattle grinds your teeth.

All is one day, the same,
As if God bid the world to exist
But for the opening of his fist

Which then closed tight and slammed,
Total and drastic as a clot.
A wild colt crops the wild weed plot.

How clearly the doctors have explained,
Although the first birds poised, they met
Their shadows, and did falter, yet

Recover briefly, before descending:
How early the gay bats come out
To wheel and flicker and cavort.

March 8   Peggy pushed her body off the ground today and screeched with excitement. Pulled herself over to Little John by doing a pushup onto her knees and then lunging forward, and kept grabbing his sleeve and hand, then talked to him in a sweet gabble. He was delighted and kept turning over to her. But then she buried her hands in his hair and pulled— we will have to teach him to punch her as he does the rabbit!

She turns her head to us, puzzled, when we say her name. Little John probably never answered to his in this way. He answers our tone of voice, not the name.

March 12   Little John's third birthday. Rosalie stayed for dinner. We gave him a new (old) Beatles record, a jump-up music box, the Spin Twins—two bells decked out as sailors that spiral down a metal rod striking another rod that rings them with each revolution—a tinkly carousel, and the poem I did last week.

March 19   Took Peggy to Dr. Riordan yesterday—"a splendid speci-men." Took Little John to him today. Much better health than in September. We need not fear pneumonia now because he moves so much. His feet were bluish; Riordan was saying this might mean a vascular problem but soon discounted it when he found a pulse in the foot. "Now you don't have to worry from minute to minute but from month to month."

March 20   Soothed Little John tonight by stroking his head. We can sometimes get him to sleep by brushing his hair or stroking the back of his head with our hand. In some ways he is closer to normal reactions now, oddly enough. And, as Dr. Riordan predicted, though we didn't believe him, he *is* getting easier to look after.

March 25	Peggy sits by herself!

April 19   There are times when Little John is crying and crying, and
we can't seem to find the right way to help him stop, that
John says with terrible intensity, "Sometimes I think this
will kill us all." As soon as he says it, all *my* helpless despair
ceases, and I become calm and certain, feeling that of course
we can go on. I told him tonight, "We just can't *think*
like that."

April 21   [From a letter to the grandfather]
Because he is eating well, he has been putting on weight,
and when I carry him, with his long back hanging down
from my shoulder, he is more awkward. Since Big John is
so tall, the bending and lifting are hard for him, and he has
been out of service for several weeks with a strained back.

To help in moving Little John about, though, he has been
enlarging the new stroller. He lengthened the back with ply-
wood, padded it with foam, and tacked on a plastic cover.
The sides have a sloped rim to keep Little John's head from
slipping off, and the back is strung with safety ropes in case
the catch should fail. We have put cushions on the foot
rack to hold his feet higher and keep them from swelling.

It is awkward for us to improvise like this, but we have
nowhere to turn for special equipment. The things we see
in orthopedic catalogs are all too large and elaborate, and
their hospitalized appearance depresses us.

One thing that we thought might help perhaps you could
find for us. A child with neurological troubles like Little
John's wants to chew things, and we suddenly noticed that
he has worn his front teeth down by chewing on his silver
rattle! Now we need something that is easy to hold, since
his grasp is weaker, and that won't wear down his teeth or
break into dangerous bits when he chews it. We think that

leather gloves or mittens might do the trick, and they would also protect his fingers, which he will chew for want of anything else. But now that summer is coming, I can't find them anywhere. Perhaps they will be in your shops for winter. I enclose an outline of his hand size.

April 22   Emily and I tugging against each other. She leaves me with the children and goes off shopping to town with my final "Oh shit!" And why? (Now I can cry.) Because Little John would not eat his cereal for the third or fourth morning in a row and last night began to wail in the car after we drove half an hour to calm him down, and he seems so much limper and less alert.

April 25   *THE MILK TRUCK*

> *The milk truck grumbling up the drive*
> *Misses the peach tree it had ripped*
> *A limb from once, but trims the pine*
> *To trembling on the other side:*
>> *Thus my weak will to my strong wife's*
>> *Shrewd sense tips up my thimble-mind;*
> *And since the child to whom the truck*
> *Drives milk wanes milkier, or like*
> *Ice cream sliced squarely on a plate*
> *Unhones his edge, milk driver, wait,*
>> *And carry home to your strong son,*
>> *Like cottage cheese, this limping song*
> *From one who drinks milk too—since phlegm*
> *And tears must sweeten the sour cream*
> *He dabs on his cracked tree's pale peach—*
> *And rips his wife back when she rips,*
>> *With pinecone pins: we tremble, each,*
>> *For love before we melt in it.*

98   And Say What He Is

April 30   A visit, this past weekend, from my father's closest friends
in New Zealand. Showing them slides, holding Little John
in my lap, I felt him leap convulsively every time they
spoke. He now can't stand the voices of strangers, after
several months in which he's been enjoying visitors.

Arthur said, looking at the thin torso and the bony legs,
"It's a wonder he can live at all, isn't it?" I was surprised,
because there seems a good deal of him there to me, until I
realized how this huge healthy farmer must gaze at this
frailty and be scarcely able to bear it. I suppose Dad would
see him much the same way.

Though he's been jumpy and irritable, he's also been very
active and laughing lately. He's had a change of medication,
and with this new one his little face tightens with effort and
intensity. The slack empty look goes. He clearly has his mind
engaged in the effort of what he's doing, and though he easily
becomes frustrated, if he succeeds, what a look of pleasure!

May 5   Dug a small bed for vegetables by the northwest face of
Lookout Rock. Resting, in the shade of avocado and
ceanothus, my back on a smooth boulder; a light breeze
that first brought and then carried away high cirrus rain
clouds and made an atmosphere like that of a Pennsylvania
spring day before rain. I chewed a small new reddish avocado leaf; it tastes like fresh grass. Felt I was inside James
Wright's poem about lying in a hammock but did not
think I would end it, "I have wasted my life." Rather—
later, as I gave Little John his bottle of juice under the
trellis—it is moments like this that life is made for.

May 12   John and I admitted our worst thoughts a couple of nights
ago. Perhaps the sabbatical leave this fall will see it through.
Perhaps the sabbatical is in order to help us enjoy him, to
the end.

99   The Life of a Special Child

And yet, God knows, it will be terrible afterward. One becomes dependent on another's dependency, on the restrictions placed on one's own freedom.

What is most helpful is that with Peggy the emotional center has shifted. I am more aware of the trials, less of the *grief,* with Little John. He looms less large in giving both joy and sorrow.

May 13   Tonight he is getting his head up high in the air again, as he has not done for some time. At first he was moving it just a few inches sideways—but with such giggles of delight. This is cruel. A few months ago he could hold it "way uppity-air" with almost no effort. Tonight it hurts me bitterly, seeing this little creature slowly deprived of his strength, his skills, his small pleasures and triumphs. When we are tired, it hurts us more, seems more unacceptable. "A valiant boy," Stella said. And why should this valor all decay in the fretting of neurological pain? "It is God's will?" A feeble answer.

May 18   [From a letter to the grandfather]

We have had a lot of people to visit this week, though not in the evenings, which are totally devoted to Little John. He has to be carried, played with, or fed from the time we finish our dinner until about ten. All our entertaining has to be very simple, a cup of tea and a scone, and when the weather is warm, we sit outside so I don't even need to tidy up the house! I find we can entertain more now I am not teaching, and since it is hard for us to get out with the children, it is nice to have people here and helpful to share our feelings with them. One of them spoke touchingly of Little John's "radiant spirit." Another pointed out that from Little John's behavior as he is, you can see what he would have been like with normal skills and strength—"a sweet *teaser."*

Even though our life has some very real limitations and difficulties and we live from day to day, the days are pretty good.

May 30
Emily (I didn't know this until today) has been fearing for two days that she might be pregnant. She has been turning over in her mind the question of abortion—which she could obtain legally since our first two pregnancies have ended in anomalies. She had begun to feel the willingness of courage: she would go through with a pregnancy if it happened by accident but would never set about it deliberately. Today she told me, having discovered her fears were groundless.

June 4
Little John on his changing table tonight, happy. I hold him, my right hand cradling his head, my left hand in the small of his back. He looks right into me with his crossed eyes and hugely dilated pupils, through which it is doubtful how much he can perceive, but he looks and looks, shifting his focus from one lens of my glasses to the other, perhaps catching the reflected lamplight. He has a look of anticipation. One can almost imagine him about to speak? I did not go so far as to imagine this, though I found my eyes building up with tears.

Told Emily, who worded it: "In even the most—I can't use the word *ugly* any more—hard-to-look-at retarded children, there must come glimpses of what might have been." And John is not "hard to look at."

The greatest satisfactions come from the little boy himself. Last night, after a quiet, happy evening together in the back room, I had washed him off, had played with him on his changing table, and for half an hour had been leaning toward him, holding his milk bottle while the music box

101 The Life of a Special Child

played "Jack and Jill" slowly over and over. And I thought, a sort of thought one hardly dares whisper, "I am near saintliness!" I knew that all I did was good, all calm, ordered, and yet flooded with love; and the recipient *and agent* of my goodness was happy.

Such moments are harder to reach in normal life, for most persons are too active within themselves to receive with Little John's pure passivity—which in turn generates on the giver's part a purer activity. But it doesn't do to write about this—it will sound sanctimonious, not sanctified.

In June we traveled north, taking Peggy with us and leaving Little John at home in Rosalie's charge, assisted by two young baby-sitters, one of them Dr. Riordan's daughter. It was the first time we had left him for so long—five days—and it went well for all. Peggy was as happy a traveler as Little John had been on the same trip two years earlier, and Rosalie managed readily with the help of her two assistants, for whom we had compiled an elaborate set of instructions.

LITTLE JOHN'S DAY

7:00-8:00 A.M.   WAKES. Should be picked up before he gets too cross. Walk him a little, give him his medicine (2 phenobarbital tablets, 10 drops Dilantin) and 7 ounces of warm milk mixed with about 6 teaspoons Sustagen. Give him 1 teaspoon Neo-Cultol laxative, warmed.
BATH after milk: wash him on his high table.
JUMPER after bath for a short time.
DRINKS juice (perhaps).
WALK in stroller, in orthopedic jacket, up the hill and back.

11:30-noon   EATS potato chips, still sitting in stroller on return from walk, parked on path beside back-door steps.
DRINKS Hawaiian Punch, then kicks on his back on living room floor for a while. Often has a bowel movement at

this time.

DRINKS a little milk in bed.

1:00-3:00
or 4:00 P.M. SLEEPS with very cool clothing. Keep house *very* quiet while he is going off to sleep.

WAKES and is turned on back in crib to play with rings until he complains.

IS CARRIED, head on your shoulder, around the garden for 5-10 minutes. Then, if warm, put him outside in front patio on foam pad. Play with him. Give him more juice.

5:00 P.M. WALK up hill in stroller.

EATS potato chips, perhaps bits of graham cracker when you return. Easiest in stroller. Likes to play teasing games about opening mouth. (Pretends to open it, then doesn't, you say, "John! You're a tease!" and he smiles or laughs.)

5:30-6:00 P.M. DRINKS more juice (sometimes). Then put him on floor on foam pad in back room. May need someone to play with him, especially game of pushing noisy toy off his chest. Should be willing to stay alone in back room from about six to about seven while you eat, sometimes longer. But then will want to be played with.

8:00 P.M. DRINKS milk sometimes about 8:00 P.M. If he is thirsty, he will move his tongue up and down in his mouth. Likes to spend evening in the back bedroom, sometimes on the bed for a change from the mat. NEVER LEAVE HIM ALONE ON BED. Drinks best if big musical toy is wound up and the Spin Twins are constantly spinning down. Get these going before putting nipple in his mouth. Be firm with bottle, but don't force him if he really doesn't want it. Makes him furious.

If he is complaining, pick him up before he starts actually crying or screaming, as he takes a lot of walking and cajoling to calm down. *Principle: Never let him get too worked up.*

103   The Life of a Special Child

9:00 P.M.	BEDTIME. Goes to bath table, is changed, kicks on his tummy a bit, hits his blue rabbit off the table, has his medicine (4 pills phenobarbital, 10 Dilantin, sugar). Also 1 teaspoon "chocky medicine"—a laxative in chocolate syrup. Bedtime is a play time, and he laughs a lot if you talk to him.
9:30 P.M.	MILK in bed with musical toy going, and if he is difficult, turn the windmill on the Busy Box. Usually drinks 4-7 ounces.
10:00 P.M.	BED. Turned on tummy, covered with sheet tucked in at foot and side and lamp turned down to night light. WEARS ONLY LIGHT SEERSUCKER PAJAMAS UNLESS THERE IS A FROST (not likely in June!). BLANKET ON ONLY IF THE NIGHT IS COOL. LEAVE HIM WITH SHEET ALONE FOR 10 MINUTES, LIGHT ON, TO SEE IF HE GETS HOT. If there is a heat wave, you will need to use the fan in his room, afternoon and evening.

IF YOU (OR HE) GET/S DESPERATE!

The hammock seems to be a success. Always stay close to it; keep one hand on it. He likes best to have it swung gently.

If he is crying and won't stop,
1. Walk him in garden if daytime. Always put thick diaper on your shoulder—he bites!
OR
2. Hold him beside the jumper harness, and let him push it (with a sweep of his arm) so the chains rattle. This usually works.
If neither of these works,
3. Leave him to cry it out in the back room or on his bed, face down, for 20-30 minutes. If he doesn't stop, or starts

up again after a period of quiet, pick him up and again try
1 or 2. We have found this infallible. He is always ready to
be soothed after a good cry.

The never-failing charmer: the game of pushing the carousel or Mickey Mouse or the white clown off his chest, especially on the big bed, where it sometimes drops to the floor
with a satisfactory crash.

Other diversions:

1. Put him on floor in his room near the blue rabbit swinging on its string.

2. Give him beads to chew.

3. Drop things noisily to the floor.

4. Go to the beach.

5. Put him to sleep in the screened crib.

He loves to be teased and *praised*—tone of voice always
counts more than what you say—or to have his tummy
kissed, or blowing noises made against it. Or loud kisses on
his neck. Also, playing "This little pig" with his toes—be
sure to go wee-wee-wee *all* the way home to his chin—and
peekaboo, throwing a face cloth or diaper over his face,
and yanking it off.

PALENESS. (A sudden, very noticeable pallor of face,
ears, and lips.) Give him dextrose and brown sugar mixed
with water to be fairly runny. Two tablespoons of this.
Try to persuade him soon after to take milk or juice from
a bottle.

July 10   As I gave Little John his lunch bottle in his room, it occurred to me that we have turned it into an "Environment"—
a total aesthetic experience that envelops the viewer (Little
John), bombarding him with a variety of sensory "input"
or "information." As he lies kicking on his table, naked, a
wet washrag is tossed on his face, towels rub him all over
his skin, he sucks his bottle's slippery red nipple to the

accompaniment of "Jack and Jill" on the blue music box with obligato grace notes from the Busy Box cranks and wheels; on a hot day he falls asleep under the fan's firm humming breeze, which shakes the straw Star of David mobile above his crib, and the Indian cloth hanging on the wall; a soft greenish light passing and reflecting from the vines and bushes outside the two windows fills the room; the lamp is switched on in the evening, the window shade goes flying up in the morning, and the blue rabbit topples from sight as he bats it over the edge of his changing table.

August 8   *THE GOOD NIGHT*

The good night
comes. Its wings
close warmly over his.
The wing case
hinges shut.

August 30   Rosalie's technique for feeding Little John his bottle: She carries him into the back room, lays him on the big bed, and settles down by him with a noisy toy she can manipulate with one hand, the Spin Twins, for instance, while the other holds the bottle. Then I will hear her warm, scolding, teasing talk, "Now John, you stop that! You drink your milk, you little rascal!" He giggles at her emphatic tones and turns his head to follow the Spin Twins, ding-dinging as they spin down the shaft. If there is a pause in the entertainment, he stops drinking. If there is a long delay, he starts fussing a bit. Then Rosalie's pretended exasperation, "Oh John, you're the limit, the absolute limit!" which cheers him, the Spin Twins start ringing again, and he resumes drinking.

After the bottle, in the mornings, Rosalie takes him out

in the stroller for his walk, so brisk despite the heat. When they get back, they sit in the cool shade by the back door, a happy pair, he in the stroller, she on the concrete steps. There she feeds him his graham crackers, which he mushes up into the roof of his mouth, and she has to dislodge them in a great sticky wedge. He pretends to open his mouth, then snaps it shut just as she is going to pop a cracker in—peals of laughter from them both. After this game I hear them conversing away, Rosalie in words, John responding to her in pleasant murmurs.

November 29 [From a Christmas letter to friends in New Zealand]

It's a strange situation. As someone we know said, of his brain-damaged nephew, you find yourself on the wrong train, but you can't get off at the station. We have learned a great deal from Little John of what is really essential and valuable in the personality, and it is not the mind in the usual sense. It is astonishing how much can exist when that is virtually nonexistent. His reactions to people are quite definite, as is his knowledge of relationships, and his feelings are very pure. When upset he seems to have a deeper sorrow, and when happy his gaiety is infectious; and he has a mischievous sense of humor.

Through a year of trial and error we had gained a steadier competence in administering Little John's medicines and in answering to his emotions. And we needed these skills, for he was growing more irritable and harder to please. Yet not only were we "managing to cope"—as our British family would say. Beyond that, the joys, buoyed up by Peggy's rapid development, were rising in our minds until by year's end they stood almost in balance with the sorrows.

1967

January 16   Last night as I fed Little John a bottle after he had fussed and groaned with John, I felt as if there is the person, the psyche, the real Little John, always there, but a cloud between him and us, so often. At times it seems small, at other times totally enveloping. It prevents him from listening sometimes when we try to soothe him, but I don't ever feel now, as we did when he lay under the convulsion, that *he* is not there.

January 24   [From a letter to the grandfather]

When he loses the ability to do something, like moving his head or holding a toy or standing in the jumper, he remembers for about a week and is very upset at no longer being able to do it, and then he forgets. It is sad to watch him during that time.

February 6   Little John more difficult again. Last night, gave him extra phenobarbital and had my first unbroken night in weeks, usually up to him three or four times. It's been hard to have him contantly starting to fuss, then wailing and crying, and bursting into a storm if we don't go immediately to play with him. His storms take a lot of walking to calm.

Our whole purpose, really, is to *keep Little John happy.* For one deprived of so much, it seems little enough to give.

February 17   This week Little John has been angelic—a peak of radiance, calm, and enjoyment of everything around him. Lay for hours yesterday, smiling whenever spoken to. All of us very ready to talk, caress, and tease him, because of his joy in it.

Peggy is now walking. She can be sweet with Little John,

bringing him toys and kissing his hands and feet.

February 27   An appalling ten days with Little John. No naps, increasing irritation, until there was constant groaning and screeching. He pulls up his legs, his face blotches red and white, and he *screams.* All we can do is leave him to cry it out.

February 28   After Rosalie finally had gotten Little John to sleep this afternoon and was taking her break in the living room, reading, suddenly she became aware of a distant voice. She rushed into Little John's room, and there was Peggy, standing beside his crib and greeting him cheerily, "Hi, Jore!"— having gotten out of her own crib and opened two doors to reach him. Luckily he was so deeply out that he only stirred.

March 13   Yesterday, Little John's fourth birthday. We had a small family party for him in the morning with Rosalie. The night before, driving home late from the campus, I remembered again that stretch of freeway leading to the hospital and imagined making the turns, left, right, then left, along to the Emergency entrance. That night the moon was out, full. This night there was an easy rain, turning heavy at times. Emily yesterday afternoon had been thinking about the day of his birth, sad and depressed.

March 21   Drove to the medical school for Dr. Meredith to give Little John a checking-over, our first visit since August 1965. Waited outdoors in an empty playground of her new clinic. At one point we heard gunshots, then a bugle call—taps. Across the road is a cemetery. Somewhere, among the smog-stunted trees, some old—or new—veteran was being buried.

   The examination was not eventful, except that when Little John, his face squashed into the mat, rolled his eye-

109   The Life of a Special Child

ball upward, as he has been doing, they seemed to think he "was not with us" for a moment—perhaps a mild seizure. He is to begin another sedative, Gemonil, that is more precise at controlling small seizures. This in addition to the phenobarbital (sedative), the Bentyl (for stomach spasms), and the Seconal (for sleeping).

Dr. Meredith remarked on his considerable regression since she saw him last, and reiterated, for a new young resident assistant, the *enigma:* how he had seemed almost normal when she first saw him, and was able to make some progress the next year, though slow, until the convulsion. She was interrupted by a phone call. While she was away, a long time, we mentioned to the resident that we couldn't have any more babies because it was genetic. "Oh not at all," she replied, "there's no real evidence for that." Dr. Meredith, returning, agreed, which surprised us after her last report. There are no important congenital marks of anomaly that would point to a genetic origin, she said, except for the epicanthus folds—) (—at the inner corners of his eyes and a "primal crease" in the palm: "But we felt it not right to go through the anxiety of another pregnancy when we didn't know."

Toward a definite diagnosis they could still do some blood chemistry (amino acid) studies, chromosome tests, and, when he was no longer "aware," a brain biopsy. But he remains unique and baffling, and therefore the future is not at all clear. Since they don't know the causes (etiology), they can't compare him statistically with other cases for prediction (prognosis). "A lesion must exist in the brain" is the most they can say.

What bird pursues its shadow
Down the rolled valleys of your brain,
No specialist presumes to explain.

During their examination he smiled several times at Dr. Meredith. "A very happy child," she remarked. And when the resident checked his chest, he giggled, and she laughed, "He's ticklish!"

"He used to be very beautiful," Emily said while Dr. Meredith was away.

"He still *is* beautiful," the resident answered.

Afterward, driving home, Emily said, "I didn't feel, this time, that they were taking him away from us and doing things that we didn't want him to have to suffer."

*

[From the report of the examination, Dr. Meredith to Dr. Riordan]

> Diagnosis: General hypotonia and retarded development.
> Etiology: Unknown.

In the last two years this boy has been progressively going downhill. His general health has been quite good, but he is now unable to chew, is taking only milk fortified by Sustagen. Physical examination shows a long thin boy who appears quite well nourished, is able to watch objects, smiles appropriately, and pays attention to sound.

I am sure that if an electroencephalogram were repeated, greater abnormalities would be found than those seen in 1965, and it would be of interest to have this done, but it is of no consequence in the handling of the case, I am certain.

For the present the family are able to manage quite well, keeping the child at home, and since the life span would certainly be expected to be limited, I see no reason to make any other suggestion at this time.

March 23

Holding John on my knees in the early evening, I was thinking: How *proud* we are of him! The thought was specific, related to his performance at the medical school. Anticipating, I had feared Dr. Meredith might be rather upset to see him so much less capable than two years ago; what came out instead was *her* pride in him also—"He's such a happy child!"—and perhaps in us, for helping him be so happy.

March 25   Mani, now eighty-three and quite frail, was driven up by a friend for a brief visit. She loved seeing both children. We had feared it would be hard for her to accept an adopted child, but Peggy captivated her. They got on so well that Peggy cried at being parted from her at bedtime.

March 30   What is pretty and what is interesting are identical for Peggy at twenty months. How is it that we let them split and separate, like two layers of laminated wood, the one narrowing down to a mere veneer, the other thickening into the "useful" substance which bears all the weight?

As spring wore on to summer, our routines with Little John continued much the same. Late in April, however, our professional expectations were abruptly jolted by word from the university that I would probably be receiving a terminal appointment the next year. "We're free!" I thought at first, but on a benign day, with the wind working easily through the fresh avocado leaves and the creek at the back still running solid and full, it was painful to think that we would be leaving, almost certainly for good, a place that had been so good for Little John and ourselves.

Luckily I had been offered a visiting year at a college in Colorado, and now I accepted it. The worst part was that we would lose Rosalie, who felt she could not leave her two dependent brothers for as long as a year. She would stay with us there until Christmas, though, which would allow us time to find a replacement. What gave us hope that we ever *could* replace her was the fact that Little John's care was growing easier, and thus Rosalie's special talents for coaxing him out of the private tower into which he more and more was withdrawing were no longer so essential. An energetic high school senior, Julie, had begun helping us on weekends in the spring and soon learned to manage both Little John and Peggy for a few hours at a time.

Besides the move, there was another large change in the pattern of our lives. We had been feeling it would not be fair for Peggy to grow up as an only child, and during the summer we went again to the adoption agency. Before our move we brought home a little boy, whom we named Andrew. Peggy acted a bit scared, as if we had brought some terrifying wild animal into the house, but we gave her a stuffed bear, bigger than the baby, for her to adopt, and she held it tight and made it her constant companion.

Then from the university came a change of heart: they would give me one more year for a chance at tenure. As we prepared for our leave of absence, we determined to enjoy as much as we could the flickering light and shade of our house and land and trees. Through the summer we watched our three children proudly.

The more Peggy grew, the further she surpassed Little John's early achievements, *thinking,* as well as moving, as he never could. *Bye-bye,* for instance, which he could once express by waving his arm in response to our urging, became for her a concept: "Bye-bye water," she said as she opened the drain, "Bye-bye strawberry," as she popped one in her mouth, or "Bye-bye open," as she closed a container. At the table once when the petals suddenly began to fall from a rose, she tried to put them back on. Always she was seeking to *act,* not merely respond.

August 1
Andrew likes to watch Peggy, but he's bored with his crib and infant seat. With his extraordinarily taut muscles he is the exact opposite of Little John's hypotonia. And he's so intense in everything he does, where Little John was contemplative, an observer. Peggy perhaps recognizes this difference; she kisses and hugs Andrew gently at first, but quickly she can get violent about it, and she will squeeze his feet painfully, which she has never done to Little John.

August 7
Walking Little John tonight to soothe him after being out late at a farewell party for John and me, I felt: Here are

the *verities*. During much of our lives we don't have so firm an anchor; at the times we do, we are lucky. Our view of the world is tempered, we are brought down to solid realities, out of the brittle intellectuality indulged in by some of our companions this evening. In Little John a vision of the beauty in simple things is opened up to us. How we treasure his soft cheeks, his blond hair, his tiny emaciated wrists and nerveless fingers, the tan on his tummy. These are the verities, though fragile, temporal, fleeting.

August 12 To the "o-shun," as Peggy calls it. She looked like a Renoir child, pink cheeks flushed, large blue eyes bluer than the sea, hair in dark tendrils, and shouting with laughter. John held Little John to let his legs be splashed by the waves. He can't lift them to kick now, or keep his head from sagging forward. But he laughed and laughed at the white froth and turbulence and then the splash and *whish* as he got wet.

August 15 How Little John thinks: When he hears the face cloth being squeezed out in the basin of water, he grins and flutters his eyelids rapidly with delirious anticipation before the wet cloth is flapped open onto his face, and he opens his mouth to bite into it and suck the liquid.

August 18 [From a letter to the grandfather]

We have rented in Colorado what the realtor calls "the prime house" in town. Besides being well heated, sunny, and well equipped, it is on the edge of a large mountain park where the deer look in the windows. We will make a leisurely drive through the Indian country, in the oversized station wagon we have bought to carry ourselves and Rosalie plus the three children and our essential equipment. A former student of John's, Steve, and his wife, Ann, who have been helping us in the garden and with the baby, will drive our small car across, in return for their expenses and return fare. We will need two cars there since we must always have an emergency vehicle on hand for Little John.

It will be a hard trip, and we have been desperately busy getting ready to leave. Rosalie and I have had to clean and pack as well as look after the children. Our old friend Christie has been a great help, driving her daughter over to work for us and often staying on herself as well. Andrew has been extremely unhappy with stomach pains, but Dr. Riordan says, "It will get better, Emily. After all, it can't get worse!"

August 19   Andrew and his daddy were up from 12:30 to 2:00 last night, after a long deburping. I would doze and wake, and hear them conversing, Andrew cooing and squealing. "I thought, as long as we were up, we might as well get better acquainted," said John.

August 25   Dr. Riordan came out to the house this evening to check Little John before we leave. Did I want to see how to tube-feed him? What could I say? So he pushed the tiny clear plastic line into one nostril, and Little John screeched and arched back, shaking his head to escape it. When it was all the way down, he was less violent, but still bawling. Riordan asked me if *I* wanted to try it. I didn't. "Now on your trip if you have any kind of emergency, you know what to do," he said.

"*He'll* be all right," he assured us as usual. But the feedings have been much harder lately. I hear Rosalie scolding him, "John!" with only half-pretended exasperation as he lets the bottle slip or stops sucking and a huge mouthful of Sustagen milk rolls out and down his cheek.

September 6   Today we were supposed to leave, but Rosalie, carrying

115   The Life of a Special Child

Little John, tripped on a loose mat, fell, and dropped him on the back of his head. She was badly scraped, and he screamed and cried, and then went deathly pale, as during his old pale spells. The gray look was almost corpselike, given the fragility of his flesh. After some minutes of weeping, all of us terrified, we drove him in to Dr. Riordan— thank God, Christie was here to take over the babies and comfort us. By the time we reached town, Little John's color had returned, and he was cheery. But Dr. Riordan said to me, "A child like this reaches his apogee, and then there is nothing to be done." He has never spoken in those terms before. We have been worried already that Little John may have reached his peak this summer. There is no doubt he is much thinner, drinks only two bottles a day instead of four, and he hasn't been strong enough to lift his hand to his mouth to chew his glove since early summer.

We leave tomorrow. Pray that there be no breakdowns, no disasters. There's a lot of empty hostile country between here and Colorado.

The next day we left. After a hard afternoon's drive we paused at the edge of the desert, in a friend's house, for dinner. Out on their lawn we had just coaxed Little John to begin his bottle, when a frightening hiss and roar broke over us as a battery of automatic sprinklers switched on, dousing and terrifying him. After that he refused to drink at all; the country had already proved its hostility. We ate in continued confusion, and in the dark we drove on into the late summer desert. At Needles the temperature was $110°$, but while we were driving, the car's air conditioner kept Little John—barely—comfortable.

Eventually we reached the unmatched splendor of Arizona and New Mexico—the great open skies above the long ribs of red rock and broken mesa, the piled thunderheads drifting across, the lines of small yellow sunflowers along the roadsides. We could see all that beauty out our windows, but we could only wish ourselves done with it sooner. It took us nearly six days to make the trip.

Only four or five hours in the middle of each day could be used for driving. Each evening we had to unload the car, mix Andrew's and Little John's formulas, set up the cribs, wash the day's dirty bottles, bathe the children and perhaps ourselves, and somehow get our own dinners. Each morning we would reverse the procedure, like a movie running backward. It was almost impossible for Little John to drink or sleep while we were moving, and he grew more tired and irritable daily. At night he would wake with powerful spasms in his legs, and we would take turns walking him and trying to sleep, exhausted ourselves.

Only once did we stop and rest, with friends at Jemez Pueblo. For a whole long Sunday afternoon Little John slept on their old four-poster bed, his face peaceful for the first time, while we walked around the cornfields at the edge of the pueblo and chatted and relaxed. That evening, sufficiently restored to endure the two remaining days' drive, we set off for Santa Fe.

September 14   [From a letter to Christie]
The house is magnificent. It sits under a huge rockface lichened with yellows and greens, and at the edge of the garden the wildflowers and grasses blend into our lawn. Below us stretches the town, and the prairies roll out in waves to Kansas. Our seclusion on the mountain will help us to keep away from colds and infections, as at home, but here we are only five minutes' drive from town. Huge windows face in three directions—north and south to the diminishing slopes of the Rockies, east to the town and the plains, where giant outcrops of granite catch the last light when all else is in shadows.

September 16   On the mountain, on a Saturday night, we are listening together to a fine music station, Emily giving Little John his evening bottle. She holds his left hand in hers and strokes the back of it with her thumb. He finishes drinking.

117   The Life of a Special Child

She wipes his mouth, and he gives a sly smile, rolling his head a little, and flexes his muscles, straightening his legs out. His right calf and thigh seem thinner than his left, and its knee swells markedly, but the curve in his spine has grown no worse. He has been happier all day than for a long time. And so have we, both because of him and because this house is big and roomy and not ours to worry about. A holiday atmosphere—Rosalie has bought jeans and moccasins to wear horseback riding at the department picnic tomorrow.

September 18   Met the children's new doctor today—MacAlester, recommended over the phone by Dr. Petersen of the Children's Hospital, to whom we had a reference. He introduced himself, shook hands. Quiet, with a sense of humor. Grasped the situation with Little John immediately, made a few suggestions—all of us to have throat cultures, and Little John to have antibiotics whenever a cold crops up in the family. He teaches one day a week at the medical school in Denver. The Children's Hospital is excellent, he assured us.

*

Walked down to campus today, wearing hiking boots and a wool shirt to the department meeting, which I think disconcerted some of my new colleagues. Not my office mate, a witty fellow, who, along with a bearded chap—Bill Bruce? Bruce Bill?—invited me to join the department basketball team, which practices each noon hour.

Sunday,
September 24   Two days past the equinox, and it's autumn. The mountain aspens are turning, we read in the paper.

John would not drink this morning. I tried him once,

118   And Say What He Is

twice, a third time. Stopped once by Peggy tripping and saying "Oops!" I was very angry. But the third time it was the thing inside him, riding his nerves, spurring his hips and legs, that stopped him. Even Sergeant Pepper, at his height of delight—"Will you still need me?/Will you still feed me?/ When I'm/Sixty-four?"—could not please him. My grief grew very great. Outside, I walked him on my shoulder through thickets of grasses and weeds whose names I don't know, with masses of grasshoppers and cicadas, and I could voice it, there, to that alien mountainside.

We drove up the canyon seeking aspens in color. Stopped off to meet Lawrence and Wendy, friends of people we know in California, in their canyon home. They are solid, bright, steady, and somewhere in the near background I felt some great sorrow. Home, we fed John a little milk, then put him to bed happy. We talked of what must be coming, the need for tube-feeding.

*

Tonight John called me to look at Little John. He had been trying to feed him a bottle, and from the soaking cloth around Little John's neck it was clear he had swallowed none of the milk. John was talking with a high-pitched note of exasperation that gave way to terror. Little John was very pale and thin, scarcely moving—an ominous stillness.

"This is a crisis," John said. "Phone the doctor."

So I did, and said to MacAlester, "I think we should begin tube-feeding. Do you?"

"Yes."

"Well, Dr. Riordan showed me how. Shall I just go ahead?"

"Yes."

I was hesitant because I was remembering Riordan saying

long ago that when a person gets all stuck full of tubes and he can't move, he has no human dignity left, and it's not worth living like that. "Well," I said, "he's so lovely still, so responsive, it doesn't seem right to just let him fade out, does it?

"No, it doesn't," he agreed.

So I got out the little tube and moistened the tip with Vaseline, and John held Little John's head still. While I threaded it in through the nostril and down the throat, he twisted his head away but lay quiet when it was in. I syringed some milk down, and he seemed livelier at once. He has been starving to death! His abdominal cavity, which had been barely a sheet of skin stretched between ribs and pelvis, filled up tight and plump. It was done, and once done could be done again.

**Monday,
September 25**

This morning we phoned Dr. Petersen at the Children's Hospital, telling him briefly that Little John seemed less well than when we phoned before. He told us to bring him to their neurology clinic tomorrow. At the least they should see what he is like now in order to make comparisons later.

**Tuesday,
September 26**

At the Outpatients Clinic we were first seen by an intern named Brier, who asked a lot of officious questions and bragged of having found a diagnosis that other doctors had missed—holding out hope of a solution to us and then, when we weren't interested, acting a bit like God when someone declines the hope He offers. He went away to check the records with the neurologist; came back, subdued, with Dr. Petersen. No more talk of diagnosis, and instead: "We think you are doing everything that can be done for him."

Petersen, who looks like a movie star playing the role—thatched hair, handsome—has an air of control and authority, not simply competence, yet with a direct and immediate sympathy and kindness. Since his specialty is newborns, he was going out of his way to come down and meet us. He did not want to bother Little John by giving him a second examination.

After seeing the neurologist, we came home oddly relieved, almost happy, at having such an excellent hospital only thirty minutes away. They really want to help a child, we felt, not merely to diagnose or study him. Even the nurses were kind, and observing Emily's difficulties with the syringe that feeds into the tube, the head nurse went off to the supply room and found her another that is easier to use. We felt a remarkable sense of *supporting* care.

Wednesday, September 27   There are all sorts of mechanical complications with tube-feeding that we are slowly learning to master: rinsing it out to prevent the milk from curdling and blocking the tube inside his stomach; getting the right measurement on the tube so it is not pushed in too far; keeping the external portion of it out of the way. MacAlester said taping the tube to Little John's nostril to keep it from slipping, as they do in hospitals, when the tube is temporary, and then ripping it off each night, would cause terrible skin tenderness. So we loop it up to his forehead and attach it with a small strip of adhesive tape to a large piece that can be left on for days at a time. Then we coil up the remainder, tie it with a pipe cleaner, and tuck it under his little sailor hat. It looks so sweetly goofy, his own comic personality coming through even in this extremity, and the tube is less fearsome to look at.

*

Little John's weakness required another adjustment today.

The back of the stroller is down almost flat, and with its extra length it is easily tipped backward. I have counter-weighted the front end with a squarish stone wrapped in a newspaper and tied firm with twine. It's quite a vehicle now, a formidable machine!

Friday, September 29

"I'm brokenhearted," John said last Sunday when Little John would not eat. Tonight I looked at him straining to lift his head, and that characteristic tensing of all his muscles seemed like a spasm—involuntary. His eyes are shadowed and his cheeks still pale in spite of six days of tube-feeding. His leg jerks are constant. I can't see any future, and it is breaking *my* heart. Suddenly the buried grief over what might have been is coming back to life. In the market I saw a baby who reminded me of Little John—long spiky hair, blue eyes, that quiet poise he had—and it was almost too sharp. When he was more with us—for he seems to have gone further off, to smile more faintly, and to laugh less often—we had so much joy in him that the fundamental questions could be set aside.

Saturday, September 30

Little John woke up very happy. He took his food quickly, and we all got away to see the aspens in color. Drove north past ranches and fields, then west up the old gold-mining canyons, still barren with tailings after a hundred years, to Central City, and north along the range. Found a lovely spot to picnic beside a stream. The aspen leaves shake and shimmer in the faintest breeze, shooting out pure gold light. We could not be peaceful, though, feeding Little John with the tube and Andrew with a bottle, and Peggy chucking stones in a pool, needing to be watched.

Back home, I had to give Little John a prolonged enema. His intestines were stuffed with huge hard pebbles all the way up to his ribs, and during each dreadful evacuation he

cried out with pain. After this ordeal he retched and fell
asleep on the table, exhausted. Later, when we tried to
tube-feed him, he vomited; it was terrifying to see the tube
come looping out with the gouts of milk. Now we have put
him to bed. Presumably he will sleep. His color and skin
tone are good, despite the vomiting.

We should have realized sooner that he was getting blocked
up, but it's hard to keep track of all the new problems at
once. It was complicated enough getting those meals into
him, forgetting that he would need to get rid of far more
than in the days and weeks before. We don't know what
to watch out for until it has happened.

**Sunday,
October 1**

A day of grief and fear. Little John was fed a small amount
every two hours to avoid the strain on his digestion. After
each feeding he fell asleep immediately. Having roused himself so briefly, to fall back so quickly, was the most alarming symptom. At midday, in panic, I phoned Dr. MacAlester. He was off duty, and his substitute refused to come out
to the house to see Little John.

In the afternoon, though, he slept longer, more like his
usual nap, and we felt relieved. He woke gray and distressed.
But this time the food, a richer mixture, brought color to
his cheeks like a transfusion. We fed him again at nine, and
he seemed more awake, and his color even better, so we
did not call the doctor again.

**Monday,
October 2**

This morning he seemed again to fall asleep after his
meal, but fifteen minutes later he was awake. Phoned Dr.
MacAlester: "If he does not pick up, maybe he should be
in Children's."

"But that would be the end."

"Well, if he does not get better, if he gets weaker, that
may come to pass."

123   The Life of a Special Child

I walked him, crying, in the sun and warm wind. He's more a part of nature than we, more responsive to its seasons, his heart beats closer to its rhythms. Winds and sun breathe strength into him. He may know that this is his time, before more horrible difficulties begin. Let us not hold him back if his spirit knows. But if he can fight a little longer, then hold on, Little John, stay to comfort us, give us more time.

Last night he really smiled as John swung him gently on his shoulder, and during the day, in those brief periods of consciousness, there was the edge of a smile at the corners of his mouth when we walked him. Never, even at the worst, has he gone right away. His own self is still there, and he is so beautiful it breaks me.

The gods have been generous; they have given of themselves in Little John. But they are capricious too. We have him still because we have stayed with him; his spirit holds on to the world through us. In hospitals he always goes away. At Children's the other day I looked out the windows at the trees, knowing they would soon be leafless, and I knew that if we had to come back later, all the bright paint and kind nurses would count for nothing, only the bleak, bare winter outside.

11:00 A.M. Now he is asleep, and his cheeks are flushed. Why are we so unready? We have had two and a half years to prepare for this, and it comes on us as if it is all new.

3:15 P.M. I wonder at our coming to Colorado—why?

Little John seems cheerier, but the gagging and coughing when the tube moves in his throat is constant. How long can he stand the mechanical complications, the mucous that collects in his nose and throat, the problems of evacuation? If it is his time, we would be cruel to wish him longer.

9:15 P.M. As the afternoon wore on, I talked to John outdoors. Little John lay on his mat in the fresh air while storm clouds blew up and over the mountain. We decided to take a movie of him in his funny hat, and as the camera started whirring, he began to smile. John walked him through the grasses, and he smiled more and more until he was almost laughing. He did not drowse again until bedtime. After his evening meal he looked fine—cheeks pink but not flushed, eyes clear, and above all a calmness in his face which was not languor. Whenever John picked him up, he giggled, his little indrawn squeak of a laugh that we haven't heard for a week. Who knows? For these hours anyway, he was happy.

Tuesday, October 3

Today he laughed all day long, as if he were saying, "I'm glad to be back, I didn't really want to be gone after all." Everything seems to have a fresh taste for him after nearly being lost. We are jubilant and don't count the future. We are grateful for days, hours even.

*

He looks stronger. Only when actually being fed did he cry. Laughed—roared—whenever I carried him, or danced him to Beatles music on my shoulder. Beamed with pleasure at being put in his stroller and rolled out on the bumpy lawn. It's as if he knew he had passed through a dark tunnel, where there had been silence, and he had come back again into the noises of the world.

Mani phoned this afternoon. "How is Little John?"

"He's much better. Himself." I feel, this evening, her prayers in the air, right here, around us. Even asleep, he looks happy.

Thursday, October 5

Little John's ribs are covered again, and his cheeks are filling out. He gets feistier by the day, is less enthusiastic about convalescing, and angrier about the tube; he sobs and wails when it is being put in, and all through the meal.

During the crisis the thought came, unasked, "Now we will be free." We have always imagined, without saying it, that some day we would be free to travel, to do more things, and so we could stand these restrictions and limitations. But now that idea is bitter; freedom is not what we thought. To set a trip to Europe, say, against his life!

**Friday,
October 6**

You see (I have to remind myself), what we thought, even five days ago, was that this was the end for Little John. "He's a goner."

Now he seems to have gained five pounds, to be solider, tougher, more muscled than for months—all summer.

He cannot swallow. The tube is all. Yet his spirit is wild! He's angry whenever we feed him.

And putting the tube in! A tiger, with a fierce *growl!*

**Saturday,
October 7**

Who would believe how (relatively) peaceful we are tonight? It has been a hell of an evening, Peggy anxious with a painful bowel movement, Andrew tired because he was wakened early from his nap by Peggy screaming, and Little John angry after waking from *his* nap because he had hooked the tube with his hand and pulled it nearly out of his throat. Yet now they are all down quiet, and we have been viewing Little John's "last" movie reel, taken on the lawn last Monday. His skeleton has filled out incredibly since then—hardly the same child. Our fears of losing him have run off a little way with this week's progress.

*

I discovered today—too busy to notice before—a strange periscopic object sticking up in Andrew's lower gum and grating on the spoon—his first tooth! And he is trying to crawl, rocking back and forth on all fours and then flinging himself forward onto his nose, the absurd muscular antithesis of Little John.

October 9 Little John was radiant when we got him up this morning, all pink-cheeked and huge smiles, which changed to screams the instant we started to insert the tube; it was hard to push through his nose and throat because they were so tensed up. He screamed all during his meal and his bath and remained gloomy all day, hardly a smile. As soon as the tube was taken out tonight, he became radiant again. It's a shame. All the added weight and health are to no purpose unless he's happy.

October 10 *A second time it comes, that stubborn dream.*
He walks—not to me, not away—out through
Long, dark-green grass, half-tottering, half-lame,
But happy in an ordinary thing
His waking never did, can never do.

And now I wake, into the normal sun
Which sets the dry grass mountainside aflame
Out through the window where the mule deer feed,
Not weeping, not exulting, nearly dumb
Before the snow falls, easily, like seed.

Little John continued to resist the tube each morning, but he became more resigned to its presence during the day. His strength grew as he adjusted to the richer diet, and we, freed of some of our anxiety, could look around us. Under our windows the autumn kept leaping into new clusters of vivid color, and the life down there in the town was inviting. It was so easy to drive down the hill for a concert or poetry reading, and these were much more frequent than at home. Rosalie was living in the house, in a small monastic room down a flight of stone steps, and so we could get away for a couple of hours in the evenings. Also, the town had a baby-sitting agency whose manager seemed to grasp our situation and to select capable people to help us, thus giving Rosalie some of the relief she deserved. The town's size made it easy for all of us to get around in it, even when the snows came; the "snow-cloud," as Peggy called the snowplow, scraped the mountain road clear to our driveway, and the city streets would be clean and dry in a couple of days.

The people we met befriended us with an open hospitality that was new to us; the hospitality of California or New Zealand was neither so prompt nor so steady. The basketball team that Bill Bruce asked me to join was something of a social center, and at Lawrence and Wendy's canyon house we often gathered with colleagues for play-readings and music; and there we also found quieter times of refuge from our demanding household. Besides all this, once we had elbowed aside the possessions our landlord's family had left behind, we found we were living in a house well designed to accommodate our lives—the large open spaces of the living room and playroom for wheeling Little John's stroller, the warm bedrooms, and the big double-layer plate windows through which we would watch the unaccustomed seasons make their way down from the Rockies to the plains. Since Little John seemed to have decided to stay alive for a while, we felt ourselves not only accommodated but freed for a larger life.

October 11   Tonight we invented a subterfuge for feeding Little John! I had been plowing the stroller back and forth, wheeling him swiftly about on the slick waxed floor of the playroom at the end of each furrow, to calm him down, and was about to push him into his bedroom to be lifted onto the table, when I said, "Why not try it here?" So Emily eased the clear glass syringe into the flared end of the rubber tube, filled it with the mixture, raised it, and walked along beside me, back and forth, letting it flow, and John was quite unbothered by what has been his most tired and angry feeding of the day.

October 19   Peggy's determination is now expressed not only in the
              forceful development of her body, walking and climbing,
              but in her speech. "Pretty soon—" she says, to urge things
              to happen. When I come back from shopping, she says
              hopefully, "Pretty soon Daddy." When she wants some-
              thing, she orders it: "Milk-a-Peggy," "Soup-a-Peggy." After
              storms and tears when we deny her anything, she works
              her way out and saves face by telling us, "Wipe-a-nose."
              She's more turbulent here than at home.

              Today she called out there was an "idea" on the lawn—
              the first of the deer that the realtor had promised us. There
              have been rabbits, too, driven down from the mountain by
              the slow chilling of the season.

              Bill Bruce and his wife Lisa were here for tea, and Peggy
              was delighted to resume her role as queen of the tea party,
              as at home. Andrew slept long, as usual, all through the
              sociable hours, but we are so grateful after his summer of
              squalling.

October 22   [From a letter to the grandfather]
              Little John continues stronger, and we all revel in the warm
              sun with a touch of chill in it and the brilliant scarlets and
              yellows of the trees. When I go down the hill to market, I
              drive around a little, just to enjoy the colors and the crisp
              clean air. With the college so close, I have been able to slip
              away for a few lectures and concerts, an exciting sense of
              activity! To have everything we need in a town so close,
              and yet to live at this exalted height on the mountainside!
              We are so glad we came here.

October 28   Little John on his thick foam floor mat, happy on his back.
              We turned him face down for the first time in two or three
              months, and he was happy that way, too. He could not

kick his legs off the ground without great effort, but he tried to, and succeeded more and more, for a long while. It was "like old times," seeing him do one of his favorite old exercises, and it made us happy.

Snow in the night—we'd been up with the children and thought it was fog. How could there be fog up here? we wondered dimly. In the morning, this white stuff all over the mountain. Peggy, trying to account for it, said first "water," then "ocean," then "milk." Outside, she took up a handful, looked all around, and decided, "Mummy did it."

October 30   Andrew is a different child here. Those long days of driving from California lulled him, unlike Little John, to sleep and eat, and cured his stomach cramps. He has continued the pattern he established then of sleeping most of the day. When he *is* awake, safe from Peggy in his crib, he laughs and chuckles and bounces in the jolliest good humor.

Peggy on her toy telephone imitating what she hears us say: "Hello? . . . Too bad . . . too bad . . . oh, too bad . . . Good-bye." And "Oooh, Daddy," she calls out, "God dammit, oh God dammit!"

October 31   Little John very vigorous kicking on the mat tonight. Knocked a noisy toy off his chest as he used to, the first time for many months, perhaps all year. And got better at it, using both arms after a while. An amazing return of a lost power.

November 9   A new baby-sitter here today, a Scottish grandmother, down-to-earth—"Dorsey," Peggy calls her with affection and no ceremony—learning the ropes to help Rosalie while we take a weekend trip to New Mexico. We have been invited to see the Corn Festival dances at Jemez Pueblo.

Gorgeous day, a strong warm wind through the cotton-woods, the leaves clashing together like a thousand muted cymbals. Little John in the stroller beneath them, exultant, the muscles in his fat brown tummy tightening almost in knots as he laughed at the noise. We couldn't bear to bring him in out of the wind, although he still has the tail end of last week's sniffle.

*

This morning Rosalie put the tube in, for practice. I didn't even watch or help. Had not realized until then how much strain it is to do this each day. It hurts me to cause him such distress, and it is frightful to have the thing stick, or double back, looping out of his mouth like a snake instead of sliding down his throat. I have to admit it has changed our life greatly.

November 12   Jemez Pueblo, again, where Little John was restored by a long afternoon's sleep during our trek. The smell of the old pueblo, sweet-scented piñon wood fires, damp chill of the church at morning mass, the strange foods—pozole, blue corn bread—at each of several houses to which our hosts were invited, the sustained intensity of the ancient dances—half an hour for each clan to move all the way down the plaza and back, the vendors of food, silver, pottery, rugs; and all of it valued the more for the difficulty of reaching it.

Returned to find all fairly well, though Little John was coughing a good deal. He had had stomach cramps, it seemed, crying and pulling his legs up in spasms all Sunday morning. Rosalie phoned the doctor, reaching the substitute again. This time he came to the house but couldn't find anything really wrong. He prescribed a sedative, surmising that the tube is causing difficulties. Rosalie rather shaken.

November 21 [From a letter to the grandfather]
Today the doctor found Little John's cold has turned to a mild bronchitis. With medication he seems better already, and in a way I am relieved that he has something specific that we can treat. He has gained seven pounds in two months! The trouble is that now he is dependent on the tube as a lifeline, so with his nose stuffed up, and one nostril blocked with the tube as well, it is difficult for him to breathe. We have to keep comforting him and trying to clear his nose.

November 22 Third snowfall, three to four inches, soft and clean. Peggy pulling her bedroom curtain aside to look out: "Poor bunny. No habba fruit." Then she saw the pale moon going down the notch in the mountain: "Moon up there. Pretty soon, turn it off."

On Thanksgiving Day, in the waning afternoon, the telephone rang, long distance. It was my home department's chairman telling me that they had decided to bet on my future, recommending me for an early advancement the next year and for a permanent position the year after that; he added that they thought they could convince the administration in spite of last year's difficulties over my leave.

Then in the evening the phone rang again from home. This time it was Julie, our weekend helper from spring and the early summer, who had been considering our invitation to join us, and she had decided that she would. She could stay for the first two months after Rosalie left at Christmas, and if all was going well, she would stay on. We felt a great cloud of doubt lift and clear.

December 2 Still very much moment-to-moment living. Most days I get out of the house and go with Peggy to the park, where she is learning to climb the ladder and ride the little merry-go-round with horses just her size, and usually to the shopping

132 And Say What He Is

centers, from whose parking lots I look up at the snowy peaks that we cannot see from the house. The scale of the mountains and plains gives a sense of vastness, of freedom to move, that makes the small precise motions of our life more acceptable.

December 6   Little John vomited a little this afternoon, a great deal at bedtime, after gagging and coughing all evening. It's awful, the tube coming out his nose, and with his long limp back and sagging head it's hard to hold him so he won't choke. It's always scary.

December 12   Rosalie left at 7:00 A.M. from the bus depot. Still dark, snow falling thickly all night, up to five inches by the time she left, and continuing all day to a total of eleven inches.

*

This is a great change, an enormous wrenching of all our lives. Rosalie has been with us almost three years. But she's lonely here; even though she has gone riding and had the use of the car, it's not been easy for her to meet people. Dorsey has been her only real friend. And Little John has gone away so much more that her special skills in playing with him and cheering him up aren't needed so much. The tube-feeding is pretty mechanical, and while we have to try to keep him from crying, because that leads to coughing and gagging and vomiting, all the tricks and devices she used in persuading him to drink his bottle are simply superseded. Much of the day he lies quiet, gloomy, not asking to be played with and not responding much when we do play with him. He doesn't go out for walks in his stroller, and we can't dance him around because it jars him and jerks the tube loose. Of all those old happy routines, only the

133   The Life of a Special Child

bathing and going to bed are left. And even those are simpler these days.

December 19   Little John wakes sometimes around breakfast, but doesn't raise his voice until after we are through. When Emily goes in, he greets her with the coyest little smug smile. He enjoys being changed out of wet diapers and pajamas, and then being carried for a while before being put in his stroller. The tube has been going in more easily and doesn't usually upset his equanimity. The actual feedings are a bit annoying to him, but by whirling his stroller around the room by one route and then another (we call them the Inner Circle and Outer Circle Routes), pausing for refills at one of the Feeding Stations, we can keep his mind off it.

After his meal he is happy taking stroller tours of the house, and then he will lie quietly listening to the television— he loves the crowd noises of football games—or to the washer sloshing or the drier spinning or the dishwasher churning, preferring these, which are near the bustle of the household, to the record player in the living room, out of earshot of the rest.

He takes a good long nap and is happy upon waking. He gets a bit grouchy around dinnertime, but when we set about putting him to bed, he is all smiles and mischief and delight yet again.

*

We have a full-time helper from the agency, tiding us over until Julie arrives after New Year's. Peggy resents her, screaming whenever Lil says No. Even at two she's aware of the right to protest, "You have no authority over me, you have no right." Lil *is* rather arbitrary with her and overly nervous about Little John. Called us back from a dinner party one night because he had vomited; when we got there, she was sitting terrified by his bed, the lights off, listening for his last breath. Chris, a capable fifteen-year-old who also helps on weekends, was with her, and much more sensible about it, but didn't feel she could take charge. "I wouldn't have called you back," she said.

December 23　Andrew crawls around and around the Inner Circle Route, a voracious explorer. He says "ah da da da" in the same sweet gentle tones as Little John. So perhaps John was not abnormal in vocalizing so delicately and tentatively. Andrew wrinkles his nose and sniffs while smiling; I'm sure there was a time when Little John did that, too.

Christmas Day　The tree is up, smothered with the abundance of ornaments and lights the landlady told us we should use, and nearly fills the dining room. Peggy is rapturous about the "grangels" with little wings hanging from the branches. She pleased us by playing with each present for a long while before going on to the next. For Little John, new records and a ticktock windup clock, and as a Christmas treat we didn't put his tube in until after he had enjoyed them for a while.

During his nap he coughed the tube out. Again we left it, while we ate our turkey with Lou and Tim, a young couple from California. Little John lay on his mat near the table and kicked and smiled. Peggy staggered around the house with her new riding horse—its legs move when she bounces on it, and it jerks forward—clasped to her chest. "Not many cowboys that *carry* their horses," said Tim, impressed.

Thick snow outside, but we are warmed and expanded by the friendliness and freedom in this place. We feel keenly the triumph of having brought Little John here, and through another year, and of these other two little lives now bubbling around us.

135　The Life of a Special Child

1968

January 3   Just past five o'clock, I heard, once, the Spin Twin sailor
bells descend their spiral rod striking the side pipe: the toy
we used to feed John his bottle by. Four months since he
has been fed from a bottle, the tube providing all his sus-
tenance since; yet, *John's being fed!* I thought, the old
groove turning in my mind, the former song still singing.

January 12   Little John has been vomiting intermittently all week, often
his lunch, sometimes his dinner, even, once, the first meal
of the day; sometimes all, sometimes a little. A bug? Or the
tube itself? The mucous from the tube, or the cough mechanism reacting to its presence in his throat? Or the Quad-
rinal, which keeps his chest clear but is hard on the stomach?
It's frightening.

January 22   [From a letter to the grandfather]

     Julie is now with us, and so efficient and cheerful it is a
great relief. We are hoping she will stay the rest of the
school year. I couldn't leave Little John for more than half
an hour with the woman who filled in when Rosalie left,
as she would panic. And since we never take him out now,
I was closely house-bound. But Julie gives us so much freedom. She immediately learned to put the tube in without
nervousness, and she has sometimes managed all three
children by herself for short times.

     Thanks to her help, we can even have house guests. One
of John's college friends and his bride arrived in a blizzard
just after New Year's Day, wrapped up like Polar explorers.
Since John's back was strained, his friend shoveled the

driveway for us next morning! And Fran is coming out at
the end of the month, riding one of the famous trains before it disappears from the landscape.

The new year got off to a good start, once Julie joined us, though there
were bad days, of course, and for some reason these usually seemed to be
Thursdays. On one of them Julie cut her thumb, deeply, opening an orange
juice can in a hurry for Peggy while carrying Andrew, and the cut became
infected and flared up for months. On another, Little John came down
with a cold. And Bill Bruce's team was playing its basketball games in the
city league on Thursday nights, often very early, which took me out of
the house at one of the busiest times of the day.

January 25   Another damned Thursday. Bill on the phone, in a strange
voice, "He's all right, Emily. We've got it back in place, but
he's in a lot of pain." I didn't know what he was talking
about and thought he was kidding, as usual, but in a while
it came out that John's left shoulder had been dislocated
in the game, and he must keep his arm in a sling and absolutely still for three weeks—not to help with lifting the kids
for all that time.

February 3   Fran and her son Fritz came for a happy week. We had
people in to meet them several times—Tim and Lou, Wendy
and Lawrence—eating dinner around the low table in the
living room with a roaring fire and the snow gleaming outside under the moon. Little John no trouble at all.

February 9   Peggy has not been screaming and raging as much lately,
though we brace ourselves for rows over every meal and
diaper change. Then she asks for something quietly and
politely, and we are so astonished that we give it to her
without considering whether she should have it—a wonderful technique for getting her "slocket cookies." We asked

137   The Life of a Special Child

Dr. MacAlester if her turbulence was due to moving here or to the unusual nature of our household, and he reassured us, as Fran had done, "It's the age, the noisiest rebellious age, though not the *only* rebellious age."

February 12   A crucial day for Peggy. Before going to bed, walking up and down in the kitchen, she kept saying, "Dr. MacAlester says Peggy not have a bottle"—a piece of propaganda we've been throwing her. And then she said firmly, "Peggy doesn't want a bottle." So Emily gave her a cup of orange juice, and she went down without her night bottle, and no fussing. A brave girl. As if part of some revolutionary decision, she also rejected the big white blanket that she has demanded all winter.

February 16   John's arm unbound. So well did he follow the doctor's order not to move that the muscles have atrophied, and now he *can't* move his arm. It will take some weeks to restore its strength. But we can manage more easily without his help now that we no longer walk Little John on our shoulders to soothe him; it is too easy to bump his nose with the tube in and make his tender nostrils more painful. At bedtime, after the tube is out, he usually seems happy to go straight to bed. When we lay him down, he always gives us an immediate lovely contented smile. Fran said, while she was here, "Little John has withdrawn more into his own world."

February 27   At Julie's departure, to be away five weeks, Peggy cried. "Peggy's going to miss Julie," she said. We told her Julie would see Rosalie in California. "Julie get her?" she asked hopefully, and then at dinner she brought out one of the straw place mats that Rosalie gave us months ago and pushed another chair to the table, "Rosalie's chair," beside

Julie's place. And pointing to them, "Rosalie sat there, Julie sat there."

Peggy is excited about Little John's birthday tomorrow. She was very solicitous tonight when he cried while being fed, "Poor John, tell me what's wrong, John," leaning her face near his.

*

THE NIGHT THAT HE IS FIVE TOMORROW

This life, his long sonata,
Sustains its music,
Though the intervals, widely spaced,
Trace contours the unfamiliar
Ear cannot follow—
Like a raga taking a different path coming down
From that going up.

Now the points we place on his life line
Descend like an aircraft's flight to the flat plains
Of his brain—this Kansas where only human kindness
Stands up from the toneless horizon
To block and punish the wild skies of sorrow.

I gaze in his face, attempting to see inside
To see what is wrong, the brush
Of my hand stroking his temple and cheek,
Wary of bending the elegant dark red bow
Of the feeding tube, or to startle
His eyelids to fluttering, like a sparrow's wings
Boxed by a window
Inside this room where the melody still is moving.

139   The Life of a Special Child

Putting Little John to bed last night, saying, "It's your birthday tomorrow, Little John," I felt sad, remembering suddenly that he was born at 12:20 precisely, and on another Tuesday. "Tuesday's child is full of grace." Now here's our friend Lou about to have her baby—on Little John's day?—and that brings it to mind also. At times I have felt grieved at the idea of *five,* the year they start kindergarten. "When I am five . . ." I used to say as a little girl—a sort of peak of small childhood, the last of babyhood really, and the beginning of growing up.

*

Lou *did* have her baby today, a girl born about the time Little John's birthday tea party was breaking up.

March 15

Deanie, our new helper, is very good, eager to do any job although she is six months pregnant, and especially sweet to Andrew. At first her quietness, even silence, offended Peggy, who thought she was being ignored, but now it is an asset. She is not a third force of authority in the house, like Rosalie and Julie and Lil, and as a result, Peggy is calmer. Deanie has been willing to baby-sit at night, even though her husband has to drive her up the mountain again. Julie will be back at the end of the month, in time to let us go south to the Indian country for Easter vacation.

March 29
11:20 P.M.

Little John looking very happy asleep, half smiling, as if he were an ordinary five-year-old dreaming of ice cream cones. I cover him with only a sheet, though the moist air from the vaporizer is frozen on the windows.

April 2.
Mill Creek
Lodge, Colo.

A strange vacation! Brief glimpse of the South Park cattle country, a high open valley sodden with rivulets of melted snow. Sheep and lambs as well as cattle. Last night at Crested Butte, a gold-mining town now a ski resort, John phoned to California from the dining room of the old hotel to discover what decision had been made on his job. He found the administration had ruled favorably, "and the Department hopes to confirm your permanent position next year." Both of us after all very happy, though he has been offered an equivalent job in Colorado. We have more roots in California.

Since then we have been pursued down the Rockies by the worst storm of the winter, no choice but to keep going south and try to outrun it. A terrifying drive through narrow gorges under huge icicles and past long snowbanks posted for avalanches, the night coming on and the snow falling. We have taken refuge in a little lodge, with the snow piled up to the eaves and giant snow-laden trees all around. John is writing Peggy a story about her imaginary elephant, who is accompanying us on our trip, and I am writing a story for her and Andrew about their adoption.

*

What do we as "adoptive" parents *expect* of these children? We must expect nothing. Because we have no genetic maps for them, everything that happens is a surprise and delights us. But don't we do this with Little John too? Shouldn't one do this with *all* children?

April 3   Tonight, after viewing the cliff dwellings at Mesa Verde, frosted with snow on a chilly day, and having enjoyed the day's solitude as we drove through miles of empty country, we were not near a phone at six to make our daily call home for a report. We arrived in Shiprock at nine, tired and hungry, and found the only motel in town closed for remodeling. We phoned home; Little John had been very sick all day, vomiting, and couldn't keep the tube in. Julie was quite distraught at not hearing from us. We have had to drive on to Farmington to sleep, and tomorrow we will have to go even farther south and east before we can turn northward again, since the passes have all been snowed in behind us. We are a long way from home—two days' drive.

April 4   Down to Gallup, hoping we might hear better news and be able to stay away longer or, if worse, planning that I would fly back from Albuquerque while John drove. No beauty at all in the endless miles down the eastern side of the Lukachukai mountains. On Route 66 in Gallup, several motel owners refused to lend us an indoor phone for a collect call, even when we explained the urgency of our need. After wasting time trying to persuade them, we ended up phoning from a glass booth by the highway, with the trucks roaring by so that we could scarcely hear. Julie was off at the doctor's with Little John, and when I called there, I just missed them—out to lunch. If we had not been delayed, we would have reached them. In hell, John says, there is a special stretch of roadside reserved for the motel owners of Gallup, with phone booths in which they keep trying to call God, collect, and He won't accept the charges.

Rather than waste more driving time, we went on without knowing if Little John was better or worse. When we reached Albuquerque, I finally got through to Julie and learned that he was no better, but not drastically worse. No need to fly, but we must push along. Reached Taos after dark.

April 5   Reached home at 3:00 P.M. Little John today is much better, Peggy at Wendy's for the day to relieve Julie, and Julie herself no longer worried. While we were away, the older helper from the agency had proved most *un*helpful, shout-

142   And Say What He Is

ing at Peggy and Andrew, so that Julie had had to protect
them from her and felt the full responsibility on herself for
all three children.

Later Little John has been asleep all day, no tube, no fluids.
Phoned Dr. MacAlester. Not on duty. His substitute men-
tions that all the medicines he is taking, for the chest, the
cold, and the vomiting, contain sedatives. "If he takes too
much of them, he could drown in his own fluids." Once
again, he won't come up to the house to see how Little
John is. He does look peaceful enough; maybe he just needs
a good sleep and rest. But it is strange he should go all day
long without food or medicine when usually he demands
them.

April 15 Peggy comes up the stairs from Julie's room and holds the
gate open behind her for her imaginary elephant. "Come
on, little eldephant," she calls, "that's a good boy, come
on." Every now and then, since it's invisible, the damned
thing gets squashed. Julie once folded her hide-a-bed up
and Peggy was outraged, screeching and yelling, "You've
squashed my eldephant!" The other day she had him in the
stroller, and then of course we put Little John in on top of
him. She was furious. Another time, in Little John's room,
the light on, she asked, "Turn the light off so I can see the
eldephant. I see him in my eyes."

April 17 Little John vomited last night, but was happy afterward,
and all day today. Tonight he was very pale and vomited
again. He had seemed wholly recovered from his last illness,
but you never know when you're ahead, and any gain can
be easily reversed. But so can any loss.

April 28 [From a letter to the grandfather]
Julie is leaving again, though not for any very real reason.

143 The Life of a Special Child

She's restless, and it seems to be against her nature to display responsibility for any length of time. She is remarkably capable for so young a girl, but she seems to want to prove, not to us, but to her parents that she is really an irresponsible rebel. A student who is taking no classes this spring, Vicki, is replacing her. She seems not unlike Julie in being very cheerful and talkative, lively with the children, full of enthusiasms. She won't live in, but Deanie, though now far along in pregnancy, is willing to baby-sit at night when Vicki can't. I think Vicki will be capable, and I am not worried. We have managed so far, and we have only two months to go before we return to California.

May 3   A visiting English poet reads from his work, closing with an elegy for his first child, defective. The London County Council had insisted that he be certified and put into a hospital when he was one year old. Waiting with his mother in a drafty corridor, he caught pneumonia and died: "He probably wouldn't have lived long anyway." Emily was beside me, her eyes welling up with tears.

He is a very gloomy man—somber. Duane, who had organized the reading, brought him to our house for dinner, and we took him in to meet Little John. This seemed to make him even gloomier, although we tried to explain and show how much joy there can be in a child like this.

An epigraph from Boethius: *Si operam medicantis, oportet vulnus detegas*—"If you expect to be cured, you must uncover your wound." But do some of us, exposing these wounds, expect really *not* to be cured?

May 9   Visit to Dr. MacAlester for a checkup. Little John weighed the most he ever has, 35¼ pounds. "He's gained *ten* pounds since last fall!" He couldn't get over it. "His entire face has changed—his whole appearance is different. He was really—

starved." Right now, he has a slight bronchitis. "A few years ago," MacAlester said, "before some of these drugs, this would progress from bronchitis to pneumonia to terminus. Even with the drugs, there are problems. It's a little dangerous if there's too much mucous. You can sedate them so they'll virtually drown in their own secretions." And the depressant drugs slow the breathing down a lot. He told us not to brush Little John's teeth in case he aspirates; inhaling the liquid could asphyxiate him. And "As he grows, the medications will need to be upped to keep pace with his tremendous growth." But in general he was extremely enthusiastic, about his weight, skin tone, and physical appearance. "Mind you," Emily put in, amid all this optimism, "he's also a good deal less alert than he was in the fall."

May 12   Directly above my head, through the floor, I hear faint Beatles music—specialty of the house since 1965. Rapid little sneaker steps overhead as Peggy runs to climb the chair and watch a helicopter out the window. A child coughs. If it is Little John, I will hear quick grown-up steps, and there will be a thumb pressing in the soft delta under his chin to stop the coughing, before it turns to vomiting. Or a hand raising his arms above his head to help arrest it. The arms are very thin, and the head seems very large.

May 16   Emily is talking on the phone to Dr. MacAlester about Little John's muscle jerks last night—both arms flying up from his sides, knees drawing up too, and smiling at it. Yes, these *are* seizures, as we feared they must be. People who can articulate say the seizures are accompanied by pleasant mental images—sights or smells or sounds.

May 21   Little John has continued twitchy, in a fixed sequence. First he smiles a bit archly, happily; about three seconds later, his arms fling up and straighten, his legs push out; he relaxes; his eyes look up and to the right, the irises almost vanishing under the eyelids; he relaxes. Then, if we are talking to him, the cycle starts over.

Reading in Emily's diary for October of 1961. It seems unbelievable—how can it be true?—that she should have undergone all those disasters: the protracted, bitter labor, the stillborn anomalous child, and then coming home to a telegram saying her mother had died.

It is incredible, too, to read now of the things Little John could once do: roll over, raise his head, *feed* himself!

May 22 Tonight as I was putting Little John to bed, Peggy came struggling along the passageway, dragging and hauling the heavy step stool all the way from the kitchen so that she could climb up and ring the little brass chimes above Little John's table, to make him happy. This was, in part, a delaying tactic against her own bedtime. Mainly it was to be nice to John. So I laid him back down on the table, and she dinged them. He didn't smile, but he did jerk his arms down to his sides in a response.

May 26 Emily in bed with a severe ear infection. After lunch she felt it flaring up again and went to the doctor for some higher-potency painkiller. Bill Bruce drove her while I cared for all three children. In fact, I have had almost all the work of caring for Little John today. It is tense and attentive duty, grinding up the tiny phenobarbital pills, crunching the bigger Gemonils, slipping the two half-shells of the red transparent Seconal capsule open to squeeze and sprinkle its powder into his Sustagen milk, pouring the thick mixture from a big baby bottle into the glass syringe, an ounce at a time; and down it slides in a tiny whirlpool through the red rubber tube.

The end of a long day, my full-time duties—Emily and Vicki
both sick—having begun with yesterday's evening feeding.
Caring for Little John now is mostly a matter of physical
care. Since his cold last week he has smiled very little, usually only in the automatic cycle of seizure spasms. Tonight
though, as I was changing him into his pajamas, he was *almost* smiling—he was plainly happy. Bedtime has always
been a happy time. The mind is still there, and we can still
feel that he is achieving the highest degree of happiness of
which it is capable.

At 9:30 I check that Little John is not too warm or too
cold. His legs have cooled enough for me to pull the sheet
over them. And his eyes are *open!* He is supposed to be
asleep; he has had a Seconal capsule to make him sleep
through the night. I take some pride in the fact that he can
still fight the power of the drug. It is a comfort that he does
not sleep *all* the time, that his brain can still find sensory enjoyment in the dim light fanning from the closet onto his
face, the vaporizer hissing its cool steam into his lungs, the
soft sheet tucked up to his ears and under his chin.

One might approach a terrible moment, when there was
no longer any actual happiness in *him,* only the illusion of
it, a hallucination, in our readings of his mind. We look at
ourselves as well as at him, and we remember that even a
few weeks ago his cheerfulness was greater.

Out of this comes our resistance to despair. It is a rational
resistance, in that as long—*absolutely* as long—as Little John
can feel or "think" a thing, we perceive the rationale for all
our efforts. One is still observing beauty. If that beauty is
fading, falling from its angelic heights, so does all beauty
fall and fade. One is still observing the handiwork of God
in a human manifestation. "Poetry is not to be deceived,"
says a young Russian poet. "God is not mocked," said St.
Paul. This life is difficult, often sorrowful and desperate.

But we should not fool ourselves that it is more poignant, painful, or tragic than in fact it *is,* for it is also ridiculous, full of delight, even hilarious.

Today I wondered, struggling back to health after my ear infection: Is Little John really going very fast? And is it because we have *let* him, instead of fighting for every smile as we used to do? The two sieges of bronchitis (one just over) and the new frequent seizures of arms and legs are not to be wished away with talk and teasing. In this past year, though his body is stronger through the tube-feeding, the cerebral condition has deteriorated very rapidly and very far. Today, in feeding, he pulled his arms up with an expression of pain, quite startling. Shortly after, he coughed and threw up, the first time in about a week. He hasn't smiled for about a week, either, though at first with the bronchitis he was smiling about once a day. We have lived at more distance from him this year, and I think it is mostly his own distance, that he has gone away from us and from himself. When he was so sick last fall and when he had the bronchitis, he had to be kept quiet so that he would not throw up; parts of his life were lost—tossing him up in the air, dancing with him, playing with noisy toys; and so his responses to them were also lost.

*

Singing of Little John, we go back and sing of what we were, and of what, at root, we still are—

Words of the fragrant portals, dimly starred,
And of ourselves and of our origins,

as Wallace Stevens has it. Being made of the same hard and

148 And Say What He Is

soft materials, in more or less the same proportions, we are all one in the flesh.

And so we are connected with these two we have "adopted." Andrew's thick fair hair and warm brown eyes and Peggy's brown curls and bright blue eyes are already assimilated completely within our family—they *are* our family—*our* children in no less familial a way than Little John.

Without him we would not have needed to enlarge our family in this way; we might not have known that these two *were* our children. With him, what they have been and will become is totally different from what either of them, separately or together, would have become without him. So he has been their maker, and the maker of this family, its cause and creator.

In this large way and in many small and direct ways, Little John, the "gift of God" in the root meaning of his name, has been chiefly a giver, the center of many expanding rings of goodness, like a pebble dropped into a still, clear pool.

Thursday, May 30

Writing about him at high speed, I feel as if I am racing him to some finish. If so, we are now sensing, by deep intuition or more properly by deeply scored perceptiveness of the faintest divergences in his patterns, the coming of something ominous. That is how we felt back in October, when he *did* nearly die; we wrote much and rapidly, took movies and slides, because it was the end. And then it wasn't. All winter, on borrowed time, we have *enjoyed* as much as we could—everything: people, friends, music, basketball, television, Peggy, Andrew, snow, the landscape, the Indian world, books, the house, food, our pictures, piano lessons, poetry readings—alive as we should always be! If we are now really sensing the coming of the great fall, it must be by the workings of subtle sensors deeper than those of reason. Or have we just not reasoned it out?

**Friday,
May 31**

This morning at 9:30, when no one has yet gone in to Little John, since he doesn't complain as he used to about being left alone, it seems to me that he's *tired*, more than anything else. Tired of what? Of going on? This because he shows no signs of taking enjoyment from anything. Perhaps it is this that has made Emily feel so exhausted during her ear infection and sore throat. That it is about time we gave up, and this is hard to admit.

Well, so the crazy little cluck! Tonight after dinner, his tube out, while I am sitting beside him figuring grades, he gives a smile I don't even see, but Emily does. And we work on him a bit with our voices and hands on his arms and cheek, and he smiles four or five times more.

And then, in a very few minutes, he goes through a sequence of seizures, quite sharp, maybe two or three a minute for three minutes. So we have to wonder, was he just smiling at some little brain impulse preceding the seizures?

Stepped outside just before 9:00 P.M., still enough light to see far and clear. Clouds—"floating mountains" Shelley called them—over the plains, due east from here. They are purling down to earth in rain mist, and behind that a few sharp slits of lightning shoot quickly down, as if in imitation of the little lightnings in his brain that release the thunder rolls of arm spasms, leg jerks, and eye upcastings.

Absurd to suppose that the big weather machine is responding, as if he had sent it little signals! We endure our lives by imagining equal absurdities.

**Saturday,
June 1**

[From a letter to the grandfather]

We must be out of this house at the end of June. John

will drive the truck to California with a full load, so that he can meet us there when we fly Little John back with special medical facilities on the plane. The latter will cost the earth, but I can't see any other really safe way of getting him there—the long drive would be far too arduous now, and a train trip with the other babies would be too much for me without John's assistance. After this last bout of sickness I will not be so sorry to leave Colorado.

June 2   A colleague from California, on a trip, not having seen Little John for a year, observes, "He used to be responsive; now he's inert." I resist, almost resent, the word. Yet do I have any right to? Isn't that what he is?

June 7   A letter from Rosalie, received today: "Yes, it is sad he is withdrawing, but if it is into a comfortable world, I guess it's the best we can hope for. Bless you all."

June 11   About 11:00 A.M., alone in the house with Little John, he complaining a bit. I was packing some books in the hall around the corner, when I heard a soft thump. Curious— had he knocked something over? Went to see. He had flung himself out of the stroller, his legs still lying on it, his body draped like a blanket, resting on his head. But his neck is so supple and loose it had simply twisted and nothing seemed broken or even strained. He was silent, in no pain— not even aware of what had happened. I lifted him quickly onto the couch. He gave a big grin—and then the seizure, a pretty bad one, that follows such grins. And then more seizures. As the day has gone on, he has shown no ill effects.

June 12   After Little John's last feeding tonight, Emily checked his teeth. One of the middle lower ones was loose. She jiggled and pulled it easily out, leaving a dent in the gum and a small pearl of blood. The tooth itself very small, almost round, worn down to a nub, slimy with dirt. "And his baby teeth were so beautiful and white," she said with great regret.

June 13   What is sad: Leaving him unattended for an hour at a time in the morning or late afternoon, because we *can* leave him like that now without his complaining. But *should* we? He *is* still responding; there are faint groans, and there are the eye flutters when we stroke his cheek or temple that used to precede a smile and even, long ago, a chuckle. He is not unaware of us, but these are all we have left to build with.

And also sad: Having put him in bed, to come by in an hour and find him lying with his eyes open—for how long? That he may spend hours awake by himself seems dreadful because we imagine what it would be for a normal kid his age—one of those children who are occasionally discovered, barred and locked into cribs in dark rooms of old houses by demented parents. So to realize that it does not "bother" or harm him to be left alone takes an effort of imagination.

What passes in his mind, though, when he flutters his eyelids or lies in the living room for an hour with his head turned in one direction? Can we call this *thinking* in any sense?

June 14   Before dinner, while Emily attended the other two children, I tested my idea that we should be giving Little John more stimulation. Sitting beside him, I stroked his arms, lifted his hand, and formed it around the side bar of his stroller— he didn't like that, and twitched his feet with the effort to pull his hand back down to the safety of his chest. He made several tries before he succeeded. When he did, I said firmly,

152   And Say What He Is

"Good, John!" and made him do it again. He was not happy, but he was not blank. After letting him rest, I worked at massaging his right cheek, which feels frozen, as if with novocaine.

Why? I thought later: *Because he is a holy person.* It is to be touching a saint, or rather an angel, because saints have been sullied with a human will, the conflict of desire or self with love or others, which he has never undergone. His face has always been purely "angelic."

June 15   Dr. MacAlester remarked today of Little John, while I was in with Peggy, "He could aspirate something and be gone tomorrow, or he could live another two years."

June 18   Andrew is climbing all over the furniture, a bit alarming. He clambers on the bed in the playroom and bounces, and throws his head down like a horse snorting and tossing its mane, full of joy.

Little John still not smiling.

*

I have been reading from letters we received on his birth. There are so many bitter ironies in these happy congratulations, but they add one onto another so sharply that the end sum is sweet, and I feel again the joy we all felt—so many welcomers, for such a special birth.

Packed photographs in the evening, for the return. Pictures of Little John sitting in his stroller or his highchair, eyes crossing, but with so much energy as he pumped and turned and strained and yet could never do the things that really count. Since he never knew that, he just went at it for the joy and delight of doing.

Last night at his bedtime his legs had been jerking quite

153   The Life of a Special Child

sharply, and Emily said, "We should be prepared for anything."

June 20   He slept quite late this morning, until about 10:30. And was drowsy once he was up.

It would seem my experiment at drawing him out has not succeeded. He has resisted, twitched, and been upset, and when I have not been stroking and talking to him, he has relapsed into a greater somnolence. We simply cannot stop him from wherever he is going—whether to an absolute breathing stillness, comalike, or to a breathless one.

Sunday,   Bill and Lisa came by for a few moments and saw Little
June 23   John. We said he was less well, that he looked worried. "I think he knows more than we do," I remarked. Bill said, "He looks scared, Emily."

Monday,   Emily phones Dr. MacAlester about Little John's extreme
June 24   twitchiness. He says we can't stop it by increasing the medication. Since it happens when we go near his face, touch him, etc., it is a voluntary movement. It is his way of expressing feeling, a minor temper tantrum. He is not in pain from it; he wouldn't go to sleep if he were.

Tuesday,   Little John is calm and quiet, the hour before noon,
June 25   motionless except for his eyes, which jerk back and forth and up and down, as if exploring the whole round of their vision, and his eyelids, which lift sluggishly as the eyes raise. His cheeks and chin and eyelids and forehead are quite pink. Why? He isn't too warm, and he isn't sunburned. Emily walks by and remarks, "He is calmer; he looks content."

Wednesday,   Last night I walked him on my shoulder, the first time
June 26

154   And Say What He Is

in months, and when I put him down in bed, his eyes were closed. He seemed to have been lulled by the motion, that easy old ritual comforting to us both. How my mind leaped to the hope that we might be resuming it—though now it is back-bending, since he weighs 35 pounds and is even limper than before.

*

Today he slept late. At noon Vicki went to get him up and called me. He looked strange—rigid, stiff, with a trembling of the muscles, his eyes fixed high, open, not moving. Got him out of bed, and he began shivering in rhythmic shudders and spasms. After medicine the shivers and spasms stopped, but his eyeballs remained fixed. Reached Dr. Mac-Alester on the phone. He thinks it might be a postseizural state, from getting his medications so late in the morning. If not improved by this evening or tomorrow, we are to take him in to be examined.

At midnight his eyes opened when I went into the room. They still seem fixed, but he closed them again and went to sleep. Asleep he looks calm, not really any different.

Thursday, June 27

Sudden increase in degree and intensity of concern. Still sleeping at ten o'clock when we got him up, and his diaper was completely dry. It had been only slightly damp last night. The right eye swollen shut where he had been lying on it. His whole face very puffy. The left eye is scarcely open and looks glazed and fixed.

After feeding him, we took him down to Dr. MacAlester, whose nurse allowed us an appointment only when we *insisted* this was an emergency. While we waited, Little John twitched and groaned, and the tube backed up and leaked fluid. Dr. MacAlester, suddenly very grave, remarked the edema—puffiness—in the face, the circulation slowing down, and said he felt it was near the end. A shock—a sudden liquid pressure in the eyes. For our sakes and the other children's and his own, Little John should be in the Children's Hospital, where he can be kept comfortable. He asked, "Do you want to take him in right away or in the afternoon?" Of course we said the afternoon.

He seems semiconscious only. When I moved him into the sunlight, his eyes opened in apparent response. These movements must be only reflex, said Dr. MacAlester: "It is really bad. It might be a few days; conceivably it could be longer." We are taking him to Children's this afternoon, where they are to use "supportive" measures only—not "heroic" or "prolonging" ones.

Emily: "He seems to know what to— He had only those two weeks of irritation, and since then, the last two days, he's been very peaceful." So suddenly, quickly the mind must twist and adjust, now *knowing* he is "dying," in the sense of *right now,* not gradually as he has been doing all these years. Everything shifts slightly, speeding up, and we look out now to a point on the horizon on which we can almost focus.

He is lying on his stroller by the open window, the cottonwood tree beyond it shaking with the wind, then standing dead still with the intolerable burden of noon sunlight. Emily is sitting with him, stroking his hand. When he opened his eyes a while ago, he looked much worse. The whites were bloodshot. He was not conscious. He is breathing easily, a quiet snoring. "When I saw him first, in September," said Dr. MacAlester today, "I wouldn't have thought he would last a month. That was before the tube-feeding. And of course without the tube, he wouldn't have."

Nearly three o'clock. Taking him away. Lagging. Do we really have to go in today? How about tomorrow? Emily phones Dr. MacAlester. *Yes, today.* He could have a brain hemorrhage and be in pain, and what could we do? Driving to Denver, bright clear day, beauty of sky, a few small clouds to north and east, tiers of them to south and west, sky very blue. One look at him, and the receptionist breathlessly waves us through to the ward to settle him in bed before filling out forms.

Behind the pleasant waiting rooms, the hospital is depressing. This is an old ward, and Little John's is a grim tall pale-blue room, small window, old metal crib with bars close together, reminding me of pictures I've seen of ancient mental hospitals. Yet objectively this place is as "nice" as any. Emily is grateful for the privacy and lack of bustle—the nurses and doctors are quiet, and there are plenty of them. "Now that we're here," she admits, "I'm relieved that he's in the hospital and not at home." Still, it is hard not to feel angry at having to be here. Some of our resentment we inwardly turn on the intern with a Southern-white accent.

It is the ending of what has been living, even though that living has dropped so far back in the last weeks. And he is *still* living, lying there breathing, looking peaceful and again beautiful, clean, white, blond and pink, in the white hospital gown. As if he were in for a checkup and would come out and home again in a few days, tired from it, and gradually return more or less to himself.

"Is he normally this flaccid?" asks Dr. Michaels, the intern. "And did he always breathe that funny way, from the diaphram?"

Leaving him, we think we will come back after dinner. Driving home, we are tired enough to know we won't. At home, so we may lift up our hearts a little, our Andrew stands up and makes his first ten steps to me right along the kitchen floor!

The desolation before dusk, bringing in from the car Little John's diapers and the few things he was wearing. We had dressed him up in olive-green shorts with belt and plated buckle, bright red checked shirt. And shoulder cloths—out of pride I had carried him into the hospital on my shoulder, not slack in my arms. His bedroom strewn with the paraphernalia of his existence but otherwise empty tonight. What do we do with the *things*—save them or throw them away? Store them for the other children? Who tonight around the dinner table are saying "Me me me" in their various voices, insisting upon their right to live—this is life, we are life, this is how it goes on. If John can no longer insist, in any voice, he forfeits his right, even though we try— have tried— to preserve it for him. And we *have* preserved it, too, as gracefully as we can. But we are tired tonight and feel as if deserted by the gods.

Cables to New Zealand and Scotland: LITTLE JOHN IN HOSPITAL   CONDITION CHANGING FOR WORSE

Friday, June 28 9:00 A.M. Phoned hospital. He had slept calmly after "tolerating" his feeding last night.

11:30 A.M. Feverishly eager to get back to see and touch him. A wrung-out, scoured feeling. One avoids all trivia and moves steadily and purposefully, like an avenger, through the people on the sidewalks, the mobs of summer school students. We have left the children with Lisa so she can help Vicki with them.

1:00 P.M. No urine since 10:30 yesterday morning. His eyelids even more puffy—more edema. Some fluid in his lungs, so he is turned from one side to the other every two hours. The intern, very gentle, says they are treating him for pneumonia, with an antibiotic. Should they be doing this? Isn't it a "heroic" measure? Haven't we always hoped the end would come swiftly through some small illness? Dr. Michaels is reassuring, and quite firm about the antibiotic. He wonders if Little John is oversedated. Emily explains that he has had these medications for years, except for the Dilantin added two weeks ago for the new seizures.

We are cheered by the lack of abrupt change. Yet we have the feeling, though almost unspoken, that he may not last very long. Everything about him is natural and seems to be settling down.

Later the Medical Director of the hospital told us more. Little John probably has a demyelinating disease, and there may have been some sudden cellular failure in the myelin sheath around the nerves in the brain or a collapse in the protein structure. Children are very *labile*—subject to free and rapid change—hence the abruptness of this decline. On the other hand, there is no apparent or massive overall infection, no high-grade pneumonia. He could stabilize for weeks, even months, though also there could be a sudden change for the worse in a day or so. He might be with us for a while yet, though he may need to stay in the hospital. Two days without much change is a good sign. Tremendously lifting to our spirits.

*

Home to dinner with Lisa and Bill. Andrew crawled all over me as I sat on the grass, rolling over on me in ecstasies. Peggy watched silently from the dinner table, angry and resentful of his way of getting attention. She was much happier after he was put to bed. But Vicki says that all day, while we were not here, Peggy refused to leave Andrew's side, and when they went out in the car, she sat in the back with her arms around him. When I talked to Peggy of Little John sleeping and happy at the hospital, she complained, "I don't feel very well. I need to go to *house*pital."

We slept deeply, though John was very upset last night when we went to bed. Soon after breakfast I took Andrew out with Vicki and Peggy to buy his first shoes. He stood stock-still in them, frozen; finally, persuaded to move, he lifted his feet high in the air, taking giant steps as if over huge obstacles, until Vicki and I were weak with laughter.

*

10:30 A.M. Emily out shopping. I phoned the hospital. "He wasn't doing too good a little while ago. The doctors are in there now doing an I. V. Can't breathe very good, get rid of that mucous. *Wondered if you could come by.*"

11:15 A.M. Emily still out. I am half urging her to stay away, half hurrying her home.

We do not want to give him up. We have reached the point, I think, where we will ask for just one day, a half day, one more short summer night, one more afternoon—today, with him peaceful, quiet, us there to help.

*

Reached home to find John white-faced, in terror, "We've got to go in at once; he's worse, on intravenous." When we arrived, they were still working on it. At that moment Dr. Petersen met us, his face full of sorrow and distress; he spoke as if this were his child, his grief. He *apologized* for not having been there to receive Little John on Thursday—he was at a conference that is engaged in announcing a major breakthrough in the treatment of Rh factor births. He told us he would do anything he could. We could phone him here or at home at any time.

We asked him what we should be doing for the other children. "Do what you *must* do, stay here twenty-four hours if

160   And Say What He Is

you want, or be at home with the other children. They need us more than we often realize. Talking to them, we sometimes have to work from their fantasies. Small children often have very little real idea of what is happening." He walked down the hall with us, so distressed, so totally sympathetic it was almost beyond belief. There was no doubt that he viewed the situation as extremely grave. But we knew we had someone to lean on.

In Little John's room they were still struggling to insert the intravenous needle, so we went down to the cafeteria. As we were waiting in line, I half-noticed a woman in white uniform in the kitchen. Suddenly she was standing beside me; I all dazed. "We're short of meat; it came in too late for me to cook it, but there's cheese. Would you like cheese?" We nodded, and she went back in around the counter and made us fresh sandwiches. We began to realize this was her gesture of understanding, wanting to reach out to us, having seen the desolation in our faces. This is an amazing hospital, and very touching things keep happening here.

When we went back, Little John looked better. Face, lips, eyelids less swollen. He had been having breathing difficulties when we arrived. His fever has decreased with the antibiotics. They have stopped the phenobarbital and all other sedatives for the time being. He seemed a little more conscious, objecting to being moved, fighting a little when I wiped his mouth. The intravenous feeding had begun earlier, when he had thrown up and expelled the nasal tube, just as he always does at home with the onset of an infection. Dr. Michaels says he does have pneumonia, "but seems more alert in some ways." Fever is 102°.

*

2:15 P.M.   Nurse Joyce Grandrath: "Johnny boy, got to get your

161   The Life of a Special Child

temperature, Buster. You don't like that? You *tell* me if
you don't like it." Gives him a lemon-flavored swab to
chew, which he does, griping a bit, and twitches toes, blinks
eyes. "He wants to chew on it." Temperature is down to
99.6°—he has responded to the antibiotics! "OK, boy.
He's breathing better, too." He hiccups. Looks very clean
and plump.

*

He was peaceful, so we drove home and swam with the
kids at the lake. Andrew was very solemn, scared of the
water. Peggy would not greet us. John talked to her, then
I played with her on the inner tube, and at last she began
to smile. Vicki suggested I swim; I was reluctant to leave
Peggy, and I asked her would she mind if I went in. She
stared at the water a minute. "No, don't go." We have to
keep probing, trying to get at what she feels.

At six we phoned the hospital. He had knocked the intravenous needle out again.

After dinner, a return of anxiety, grief, fear. So at eight
we made the long drive back to the hospital. Little John
was peaceful, awake, the intravenous tube all set again. The
needle is attached to his arm, which they have tied down to
immobilize. He blinked a bit when we spoke to him. He
has a lot of wounds in his foot and ankle from their attempts
to find a vein. He is very still, eyes not moving as they were
this afternoon. It is a comfort, though, to be with him.

*

9:00 P.M. "Wee John, you're a brave little guy. You just keep fighting."
All we care about is the immediate *moment,* even though
he is so tremendously still. One more variation in the pat-

terns of the 1,936 nights of his life—a very quiet one, this.

*

It is peaceful in the hospital at night, the traffic noise quieted, the air through the open window cooling a little.

Little John is Dr. Michaels's first case after medical school—he has been with the hospital only four days! He is very gentle and pleasant, and we have come to rather like his Arkansas accent.

*

10:18 P.M.   And so we *have* had this day!

Sunday, June 30   Came late in morning, found Little John peaceful. In his room we talked with the resident, a young German, the burden of whose advice was "Don't let this boy's existence determine what you do"—an old idea we have met and resisted before.

And a new idea: that Little John's liver, since all his organs seem to be sound, could be used for a transplant. It didn't, at first, shock me to think like this, but cheered me, in a way, that he would give some other child perhaps a longer life. But the young resident may have less sense than we of the probable duration of Little John's life. Even as we were talking, he stirred, twitching unhappily, so I suggested we go out of his hearing. Later we had lunch and came back a bit sick and angry. Is our little boy now only a supply house of used parts? It seems macabre to speak of cutting the organs out of a body while it is still living. And Emily questioned him about the dubious success of such transplants. "Yes, they have to stay in the hospital all the time, but they adjust to it."

163   The Life of a Special Child

1:15 P.M.	"Your eyes are following—they followed my hand right up there," says Nurse Joyce, letting down the crib side to give him a shot. He cries out from it, more of a cry than he has made for months. And groans.
1:40 P.M.	Temperature 99.4°. "Certainly a nice-looking boy," says Nurse Harrison. His skin is very clear, pale with a flushed rose in the cheeks. He seems conscious but very frail and very beautiful.

You can see why people want to believe the spirit goes on, up to a world where he, for instance, would be welcomed by his two grandmothers.

*

John wanted to go home, anxious about Peggy and Andrew, but I decided to stay with Little John. An instinctive feeling I should not leave, afraid that the peacefulness meant he was closer to death. Later I noticed the intravenous bottle had emptied. I asked an intern passing by in the hall—not Dr. Michaels—whether it should be refilled. "I haven't the slightest idea, Ma'am," he said smugly, and went on his way. I was furious, panicked, ran for a nurse, told her about the bottle. She was alarmed and rushed to fill it.

*

6:40 P.M.   Some sort of little miracle? Emily phones me. She has talked to Dr. Petersen, who said, "Does he look better to you today?" *and,* "It's not time to talk about liver transplants," *and,* "How do you keep his skin so fine?" *and,* "If we can get him onto alimentary feedings, he could come home in a week," *and,* "How does that sound to you?" *Come home in a week!*

John drove back to the hospital right away with the children. We took Peggy in for a moment to see Little John, wanting her to share the joy, since she has been suffering from the anxiety. We were ecstatic, except for Vicki, who had suddenly withdrawn into sullenness. The children were hitting each other—or rather, Peggy was bashing Andrew all the way home—after another day, Vicki reported, of her clinging on to him in our absence.

Phoned friends with the good news and girded ourselves for moving out of the house tomorrow, as the owners were due home in the evening. Lisa has organized a team of helpers to clean and pack, and we will move in with other friends who have room. No time to think or plan this until today, when everything changed.

Cables: JOHN RECOVERING FROM PNEUMONIA CHANCE OF RETURNING TO FORMER STRENGTH

Monday, July 1

Early visit to Little John, awake and peaceful. Lunch with Dr. Michaels, who reports a startling discovery: the cause for Little John's increasing inertness during the last few months. He had become heavily oversedated, with *twice* the acceptable level of barbiturates in his blood. The cumulative rise in drugs that depress the heartbeat and breathing had led directly to the pneumonia—another factor we weren't aware of. But surely this ought to have been tested by Dr. MacAlester?

*

Back at the house, packing and moving. Driving the Volkswagen up the hill, a lovely warm day, the curve of the road we have traveled so often opening up the view of the front range of the Rockies, I felt a powerful sense of Little John's recovery—he's going to get better; we are taking him home to California! The little blue bug almost leaped off the road and into the sky.

In the house our good friends were all slaving away. Wendy took Peggy away for the afternoon to have fun. Deanie has insisted on coming to look after Andrew, though her own baby is due in a very few days, and so we were able to give Vicki the day off, since her usual jolly spirit still seems overcome. Exhausted but happy, we swept up the last dirt in the center of the dining room.

Tuesday, July 2

Little John crying a bit, irritably—"cerebrally." It frightens us to think of him like that at home. However, Dr. Michaels says they will soon start sedating him again, gradually increasing the levels to see how much he needs to control the irritation. We see that we would have been absolutely unable to keep him with us without the drugs.

Wednesday, July 3 9:30 A.M.

The little miracle continues. On Monday they put the nasogastric tube down his nose again, and he "tolerated" the feeding. They removed the catheter he has had in since the beginning, and he quickly wet his diaper. He is cranky, and everyone is delighted that he has the vigor to be cranky. It's ridiculous!

They tell us now that Saturday morning had been even more critical than we realized. He was having *severe* trouble breathing. Besides the shallowness, which we knew of, there was a period when he was taking one breath and then *missing* the next breath. The German resident, whose advice angered us on Sunday, had been working on him with Dr. Michaels, and they had both been very alarmed. "That resident is hard to talk to," one nurse agreed with us, "but he never lets up. He really brought him through."

It's not clear what level of awareness Little John may stabilize on. How "depressed," in the physiological sense, must he—can he—be?

"They fool you," Nurse Scovill says. "Just when you think they're going to go down, they go up."

After lunch, they are having some trouble inserting a size 12 plastic tube down his nose. I trot down to the traveling pharmaceutical shop in our car and bring them our box of tubes and syringes: a size 10, and it slides in easily. We have supplies that even a children's hospital doesn't!

Phone call on the ward from Dr. Petersen. A Dr. Easton from a private research center gave Little John a thorough going-over last night. He believes there are two or three tests developed since John was last in the hospital (1965) that could provide a clearer picture. Out of these might come a "definitive diagnosis," and this would have a "positive effect" for us and for them—it would mark the end of the search. It could teach them something about the disease which would be of use in future cases. "We have a *duty* to make a diagnosis." The research unit would pay for the tests, which might take only a couple of days. We agreed to see Easton and his research unit on Friday, after the holiday.

*

Home to the children. Vicki still very sullen. She only has to hold out another week or so. Why does she let down *now?* Here we are all rejoicing, and she acts as if she is disappointed he didn't die. I cooked an extra dinner for her and her boyfriend. "How's the chicken?" I asked; she replied, "Not very good."

Friday, July 5   After our hike yesterday in the cool mountain air, the forest as neat as a Japanese garden, we felt quite calm driving off to the research unit, part of an expensive private clinic and hospital. Downstairs in a cramped office we found Dr. Easton, a tall, lean man in his fifties with a cultivated New England voice that accentuated his supercilious manner.

He jumped us right away. "I believe the proper diagnostic procedures have not been followed. I am practically certain that he has what we call metachromatic leukodystrophy—"

We interrupted, "Yes, we've heard of that. They ruled it out at the medical school in California."

"There are now far more sophisticated tests," he retorted. "My colleague Dr. Bowden is one of the real leaders." He went on: "We have only a couple of hundred cases in the literature, plus another couple of hundred that haven't been written up. It is time you faced up to this and thought about your other children. You should leave him with us. We will make the diagnostic tests, and then we will run other enzyme tests. You can put him in Ridge State Hospital and go back to California. The facilities will be much better here in Colorado since your governor has decided to cut back funds for your mental hospitals. We will be able, over a period of time, to run complicated urine crystal tests and other experiments, whenever we want, that may show up all the chromosome and enzyme peculiarities. Our one hope is of someday being able to intervene."

We wondered if the diagnostic tests couldn't be run without moving Little John.

"Of course, they could do some of the tests over there, but it would be considerably more difficult. They called me in to consult; they wanted my opinion. I suppose they could do what we told them to, but I wouldn't break my back to help them out."

"If he has this disease," Emily asked, stunned, "what is the prognosis?"

"Oh, we have one family with six children, four of whom have the disease. The oldest died at twelve. The next is a complete vegetable and will probably also live to about twelve—he's been like this for two years now; he's seven. One August he was OK; in January, in trouble; by July, demented; in the fall, institutionalized. Two others will develop the disease. They don't show it clinically, but we have tested their chromosomes, and we know they have it. It's just a matter of time."

With this as prologue he took us on a tour of his research unit, where Little John would be kept for two to three weeks—at least. And if it were *not* this leukodystrophy but something even more rare? The pressures to let them keep him would be all the stronger. The unit occupies what must have been an elegant suite of rooms in a late-Victorian mansion, high-ceilinged and echoing, divided by improvised partitions into crowded little cubicles. There were three beds in the one they would put Little John into—no privacy for our grief in there. Mobs of children were riding tricycles, pushing carts and trains around, past the doorway, which had no door. It was as noisy as a playground, unendurable.

Dr. Easton didn't know quite who we were. On the one hand, we were parents of a child with a rare ailment who might be brought into his hands, and so we must be persuaded. On the other hand, we were fellow professionals— he knew I had a Ph.D., though he thought it was in engineering—and so he must impress us. And with his liberalism as well as his research facilities: "They blow up in five minutes in Vietnam what we spend in one year." Not once, we noticed, did he stop to speak to a child or a nurse. He led us swiftly back to his office, apparently taking our silence for assent and admiration.

"Now I have a reputation for being brutally frank," he said, "and I know I have just hit you on the head with a sledgehammer, but I thought it was about time someone should."

"Oh, we've been hit on the head before," Emily answered, "but we've always bounced back." He did not like that. He was very angry.

He talked about his examination of Little John. "Of course, he is *blind,* and I am not convinced that he can hear." And of what they would do in Ridge: "We would stop this nasal tube. We would make an incision directly to the stomach and put in a permanent tube so we would not have the risk of pneumonia."

"For diagnosis only it would not be worth bringing him here," he said, and repeated that if the diagnostic tests were done at Children's, he would not lift a finger to help them. "Of course, he may go sour on us," he remarked at one point, "but he could go sour on them over there also." It took us a moment to realize he meant *die.*

We were so stunned by his brutal view of Little John's future, after the kindness and mercy we had been receiving at Children's Hospital, that we could say very little on the long drive back. All we could withhold from him, I realized with a shock, was our permission. If we said any word that seemed to grant it, Little John would be whisked into the research unit in a minute, and it would be no easy matter to whisk him out.

We came back to Children's, Emily weeping in anger and horror, and she phoned Dr. Petersen from the waiting room. He came down instantly and met us at the ward. Rather hysterically, she told him what Easton had said, and more: "I wish you'd let him die on Saturday. As far as I'm concerned I'd rather he died of pneumonia than lived six years as a guinea pig with a tube to his stomach." And Petersen took it. He is a good man. He looked straight and long at us and did not evade the pain he saw. Nor did he defend

the medical profession with a noncommittal or vacuous
answer. He accepted our hysteria and understood it, and he
said, "We can do the tests for metachromatic leukodystrophy over here and have you on a plane for California at the
end of next week. OK?" And we said OK.

And then at last we turned to Little John, and he was
smiling! For the first time in six weeks it was not from a
seizure, but he *really* smiled, rolling his head from side to
side. He seemed to do it when he heard us talking—a sort
of generalized pleasure at hearing our voices, rather than
quite as specific as it used to be. So much for Easton's sus-
picions of deafness. And the nurse said, yes, he had been
smiling when she went in and talked to him, and Dr.
Michaels said, "Yeah! He's been smiling!" He had started
yesterday.

Emily told Michaels, "We've had a rather rough time this
morning with the pure scientific mind."

"Oh, I know," he agreed. "I got so sick of that in medical
school."

"If we don't send Little John over to Easton's unit," she
asked, "will that retard the March of Medicine?"

"Hardly."

He is rather a remarkable young man, has studied Zen
Buddhism seriously, and would like to carry some of that
spirit into medicine—which he recognizes, ruefully, is as
far from it now as anything could be. He even wants to
read my poems! My God, I said to one of my poet colleagues, what more important qualification could we ask
for in a doctor?

To Michaels, Emily said, "It's the idea of the individual,
which comes out of Christianity rather than Buddhism,
that makes us cherish Little John."

And he replied, "Yes, but it's not the *ego* in him that you
value." There's some essential spirit and self that is different

171   The Life of a Special Child

from the ego, and it's this, of course, that Easton's egotism ignores; or if he thinks of it, it must not be present in a child who has something severely wrong, or how could he treat them as he does?

What Easton also doesn't realize—hasn't seen, and isn't prepared to understand—is that Little John is part of, in fact the center of, a *family*. You can't just snatch this center away and expect things to hold together—if he were to die, it would be a very different absence from shutting him into an institution in Colorado and going back to California as if he didn't exist. We also object to this whole business of keeping normal children away from everything abnormal. People should not be protected from *fate,* from having to learn to live with what they are given.

And finally there is a basic opposition between the research-oriented doctor or institution and the treatment-centered one. Treatment is more of a miracle than the research man wants to admit. The researcher is the one who says, "Here are seven loaves, and a few fishes. These will satisfy the minimum daily requirements of 8.075 adults," and he has the figures to prove it. But it's the other who divides them among the four thousand.

*

If you do violence to one person in order to benefit humanity, you have done violence to all humanity.

Wendy, who is a social worker doing a project with welfare mothers who have retarded children, said, "He told you to put him in *Ridge?*" Incredulous. "Why, we don't even suggest that to our poverty mothers unless the whole family situation is an emergency."

Saturday, July 6 4:10 P.M.

When we arrive, Little John is smiling away in his crib, at

nobody We talk to him, and he is aware of our presence and smiles even harder. He has regained his sound of pleasure, halfway to a giggle on an indrawn breath, almost a grunt on an outgoing breath. As the nurse feeds him, she strokes his arm, and he smiles broadly. He stares "wildly"— almost with alarm—but at the same time he is grinning and making his happy noises. The nurses are very pleased with his smiling. They think it is "appropriate," not random but responsive to their attention.

Monday, July 8

To the hospital after a wearing morning with Peggy and Andrew. We find Little John lying on his tummy, which he hasn't done for ages, all scrunched up, having slipped off the side pillow and almost onto the crib bars. But underneath it all he is smiling. And we talk to him, and he smiles more, and then suddenly, like sunlight breaking from clouds, he is *laughing!* His old vibrant chuckle. We laugh with astonishment, and he chuckles more; then we laugh with him, and he tightens with great gusts of laughter up and down his body. He laughs at everything—at the phone bell ringing in the hall, at ice cubes crashing into a plastic pitcher, at laughter in the hall, at us talking and laughing with Dr. Michaels. We turn around from his bed and see all the nurses crowding the doorway to see our reaction, and everyone starts laughing; everybody is happy that Little John is laughing, which he hasn't done like this since last November.

Dr. Michaels tells us that after talking to Easton on the phone he understands how we felt. He really *is* angry about our refusal to put Little John into his hands. "He said he wasn't interested in the diagnosis alone; he wanted the body."

Tuesday, July 9

Emily talking with Dr. Petersen, who says, "Dr. Michaels just moved in with him. I'm willing to write him a recommendation right now to go anywhere in the country he

173   The Life of a Special Child

wants. And I think his attitude spilled over on the nurses. It would have been easy for nursing care to slip, with a child who had as many problems as John."

He's still laughing at every signal that comes in—clearly now, instead of clouded. He's ecstatic at being aware. "I don't know where he's at, but I wish *I* was there," says the training nurse from Nebraska, Miss Scovill. She wants to write a paper on Little John for her nursing school in Lincoln. "I get more of a kick out of nursing him than any other kid I've nursed."

The care here is extraordinary. Unlike the other hospitals we've seen, they are more skillful than we in keeping Little John comfortable. They have fixed his nasal tube so that it stays still, not looping up to his forehead and slipping. As a result his nose is dry—the tube slipping up and down in his nostril, causing mucous, must have been a major cause of the colds and bronchitis this winter.

Wednesday, July 10 1:00 P.M. Chat with Dr. Petersen. We shouldn't count on their pinning down a diagnosis—they are "elusive creatures." And, about our flight home, "I hope we're not overpreparing in one direction and underpreparing in another. I've gone over everything in my mind several times."

Emily is "a little embarrassed" about John's laughing so much. "But everyone's enjoying it so! I guess it's not usual for a child with neurological difficulties to be so happy. The whole time in hospital has been such a *triumph* for him; he has convinced everybody he's wonderful."

*

Duane, who has stood close during these two weeks, helped John pack the truck last night for a student to drive to California. As they went through an absurd imitation of movers in action, fitting every little box and bag into place, they were making up mad little comic opera songs: "Will it go here, oh, will it go here? Oh no, oh no, it will not go here!" But I think the Rockies themselves are dancing at Little John's recovery, the streams leaping over the rocks to join his laughter.

Thursday, July 11

A physical therapist came up to Little John's room to show us massages and exercises to keep his joints supple. "Every now and then he'll really squeeze your finger; it's surprising."

As we were leaving today, through the main corridor, there came walking toward us at a fast clip a middle-aged couple, the man carrying a boy of two or three, hydrocephalic—his head swollen to the size of a large melon, larger than an adult's head on that little body (well-dressed)—and moaning spasmodically. There are tears in Emily's eyes as we drive away, and I am sick. It is what we have been spared.

Friday, July 12

John had a stomach bug today, so neither of us visited the hospital. Arranged by phone for Little John's dismissal tomorrow morning, including supplies to be ready for us to take on the plane, though we don't know for certain whether Big John will be well enough for us to leave. Dr. Petersen has cleared everything with the airline's physician, and they have reserved us the front six seats in Economy, three for Little John to lie on, three for the rest of us. They will escort us onto the plane first, and then, after we have wheeled him aboard, the stroller will be taken down into the luggage compartment. In California they will bring the stroller up, and we will be the last ones off.

After a hard day, packing and cleaning up, Peggy frantic, Big John unable to get out of bed, I cooked a dinner for Dr. Michaels and his fiancée—an attempt at a thank-you as well as a good-bye. Tried to tell him a little of what Dr.

Petersen had said of his work, but he disclaimed it. "It was Little John that did it. He's an amazing little fellow." What *did* he do? He moved these men to supply the care and cure he needed, but without their recognition of him, would it have happened? Easton recognized nothing. Michaels saw him at first unconscious, blotchy, inert, and was able to penetrate that appearance.

If we are floating, and we are, it is not just from the recovery but from this sense of Little John's preciousness being recognized by others. We aren't fooling ourselves; he *is* a special little boy, worth all the struggle—worth it not only to us, but in himself.

As he left tonight, Michaels paused. "Oh, by the way. Sorry to end on a medical note, but the results came back today on the urine tests"—for metachromatic leukodystrophy, the diagnosis Easton was so confident of making. "It was negative—as negative as it could be."

I said, "I'm so proud of him."

Dr. Michaels smiled, putting on his strongest Arkansas accent, "Ah'm kinda proud of him mahself."

On Saturday morning, when our two-car caravan arrived to pick Little John up for the drive across town to the airport, we found that the only slipup of his whole time there had occurred. They had not fed him him for the trip, so that he could travel on the plane without his tube in. Pressed for time, Peggy and Andrew and I hurried on with Bill to get our tickets and check the baggage. Emily stayed back to give the feeding, with Duane to drive them. Dr. Petersen himself, early as it was, had come down to see them off, and he pushed the gurney and lifted Little John into the car as if he were his own child, Emily said later.

When they reached the airport, in good time despite the delay, Bill's eyes were suffused with tears at seeing Little John restored to himself and smiling. We said good-bye to Bill for a month—he and Lisa would then be joining us in California, where he had taken a job in my own department

—and to Duane for longer, without time to reflect on what it meant to have made such friendships as these in the midst of—or was it by means of?—our tribulations, or to estimate how richly these ten months in Colorado had been filled with living.

At the ticket counter we were assisted by an official from the main office, and at the boarding gate by a passenger agent who led us straight onto the plane and set us up in two rows, one behind the other and across from the galley. There we were more or less screened from idle curiosity; elsewhere that day, people peered rudely and, it seemed to us, callously, at Little John in his stroller, and abruptly we knew we had left the compassionate haven of the hospital, where not only Little John but we ourselves had been sheltered and respected.

During the flight, though, the pilot came back specifically to inquire how Little John had managed during the ascent. He had tried to keep the pressurization steady for him, he explained, but one time he glanced down and saw it had slipped away—and briefly, that once, Little John had screamed with discomfort. For a couple of hours we flew over the great reefs of red desert rock that we had driven so arduously through, those six unending days of last September. Why, we wondered, had we never realized that flying was the right way for Little John to travel?

On the descent the pressure stayed perfectly steady, and there we were in the brave new world of California. By the time Little John's stroller had been brought up from the hold, the cleanup crew had swarmed aboard like a gang of pirates. But Steve and Ann, the young couple who had driven our little car to Colorado for us, were now bringing the big one— safely skippered across by my Colorado student—to the airport to carry us home. Soon among the thousands of indifferent faces, we spotted their friendly ones, and in a couple of hours we were home, stunned by the abundance, profusion, and lushness of California. After the lean dry climate of Colorado, our garden seemed as crowded with plants as the freeways were with cars, or the airport with people. In a day or two we added other sets of impressions, of coldness, hardness, and superficial friendliness. What all of this would mean to Little John's new life we did not know.

177   The Life of a Special Child

In the evening, when the children were settled, Emily phoned Dr. Petersen to let him know we were home. He said he had felt so anxious, after carrying Little John to the car, that he had wanted to phone the airlines to make sure that we had arrived at each point of our journey—first at the ticket counter, then the boarding gate, and so forth, all the way to California. He had also wanted to phone us at home but he had felt it would be an intrusion. "If you had not let me know, I would not have been able to sleep," he said. When Emily tried to thank him, he interrupted, "Please don't thank me, Mrs. Murray. If I have done anything deserving thanks, and I don't think I have, knowing Little John has been reward enough."

The first night at home was long and disturbed. Little John obviously missed the regular turning and massaging that had been done for him so easily by the night nurses. We did our best to supply it, but for two weeks, as never before in his life, we had been watching others look after him, and now we were hesitant, a little timorous. We had lost our deftness of touch; our skills had slipped.

Besides, this was a new Little John, not the inert one who had been hidden from us all spring by bronchitis and oversedation. Here was a little boy, very lively and glad to be alive, and we didn't know what drugs he would need, how much food he could digest, or when he would sleep. As we stood by the crib, which our friends had set up in not quite the right place, we knew that, as usual, we were lucky to have kind helpers to call on, and yet also, in the end, it was our job, with our judgment and skill, to keep him alive and happy. In spite of all the terrors, it had been good to lay that weight on the hospital, but now it was squarely back on us.

Sunday, July 14   Little John seems very happy to be rolled outside in his stroller and to lie in the sun. We have set up the brass chimes in his room, under the donkey piñata, where Peggy can climb on the cribside and reach up to "ding John's bell." She is delighted to have him home—sat beside him on our bed last night and talked and smiled to him. "The cruckets are singing," she told him. "John, the cruckets are singing a song." Since he smiles in response, it is a pleasure for her to talk to him.

Dr. Riordan comes out to visit, toting his brown alligator bag and wearing a baggy blue blazer, yellow slacks, black loafers—a Californian. His mind is full of technical reading; he is very much *up* on the dangers of oversedation, and we need not fear that he will let that recur. "Keep changing drugs," he says. "Try wine for a week instead of barbiturates. That's a much safer sedative." But also, when we spoke of the physical therapist's suggestions, he told us, "You know as much as anyone about physical therapy for John"—which is not true. We learned so much from the nurses in Children's, though they too learned from us, and we wish we could still turn to them for advice and reassurance.

July 17
Now that we have him again so enjoying his life, we are thrown into a new *present* that is also a long and old *past* —the way he used to be, and hadn't been for a year. Time had been aging rapidly before our eyes. Now suddenly, a jolly young blade again, he is switching and flicking in the green rooms of summer. The *seriousness* eases. I thought I was taking notes on the last act of a tragedy, and here it is turned upside-down into a kooky comedy of belly laughs— dinging chimes, ticktock windup clocks, Frère Jacques music boxes, sun flecks on the mat under olive trees, everyone *making a joyful noise*—when we had anticipated a dirgelike drawing out into silence.

*

Tim and Lou, who got to know him in Colorado only as he was growing more listless and inert, are here and are amazed. The first time Tim saw him, Little John was in bed. Tim approached hesitantly, softly, not to disturb him.

179 The Life of a Special Child

He was halfway across the room when Peggy rolled the closet door shut, and Little John, as he does when he hears that noise, burst into a radiant smile, and then into belly laughter. Tim stopped and stared, an equally radiant smile spread on his face, and he said, almost incredulous, "I've never seen him do *that* before!"

*

A friend asks, in a note, "Are you a receiver of miracles? I think so. I feel you are blessed."

Saturday, July 20

The isle is full of noises—bird song, especially; and today the crazy goof is giggling and chuckling at any laughable noise, that is, *any* noise. A big helicopter chuttering toward us: buckets of laughter. Emily calling happily from outside his window, "Hi, Little John!" knowing that as he hears her he will smile, and then she rings the Indian cattle bells, which he used to yank at the end of his run in the jumper track—a lovely ripple of graduated tones for his pleasure.

She calls me in from the study to see him raise his arm and *straighten his fingers*, which have been tightly curled, or loosely closed, for months. Amazing. Today I came upon my old poem to him at four months, recommending that he become a physician. A beautiful irony, for he *has*, despite his handicaps, learned to cure and heal with sure touch, and with his voice. And out of him has flowed a wisdom.

Sunday, July 21

We feed Little John a little late, after feeding him last night a little early, and his arms and legs are drawn up tighter, joints stiffer, and he is crosser than on any morning since we came home. His schedule must be kept more strictly. Also he had not been turned during the night; usually we are up to him three or four times, massaging and stretching his joints and turning him from one side to the other. Keeping him on an even keel has been taking the persistent attention of one person, while the other—for part of the day a helper, for the rest, one of us—has been occupied with the other children. Can we keep this up when school resumes and I have more outside duties? We must believe it will be possible because all things are possible. Who could have imagined, watching Little John's long decline in Colorado, that we could *possibly* have him among us here as we do now—even more responsive than a week ago, because now he responds negatively as well as positively?

Monday, July 22

In the newspaper, a front-page story and photograph of a two-year-old girl who has survived for a year with a liver transplant at a Denver hospital. The parents say—have they been coached to say?—that for the sake of medical progress this is a wonderful thing, a new record. But they also say, "The bad days stand out. There were more bad days than good ones. But we hope it will be the good days that we remember." The girl will die very soon, of a cancer.

Tuesday, July 23

The noises of the house drift over to my study across the asphalt. They are a little jammed, as if the people are too close together—which they are. Vicki arrived last night, driving our little car from Colorado, and had to sleep on the living room floor. Nowhere else to put visitors, and we need visitors. Also we need a girl to live in and help with the children, and so we need to look for a larger house.

*

A checklist above Little John's bed:

☐ 1. IS HE TOO HOT?
Feel. See (red splotches).
Remedy: Cool him down, with wet cloths if necessary.

TALK TO HIM

☐ 2. IS HE WET?
Feel. See.
Remedy: Change his diaper.

TALK TO HIM

☐ 3. IS HE TOO STIFF?
See. Feel.
Remedy: Massage his joints, move his arms and legs up and down, rock his hips from side to side.

TALK TO HIM

☐ 4. ANYTHING ELSE?
Tube stuck in throat (possible).
Diaper pin sticking him (unlikely).
Foot caught in side of crib (sometimes).
Arm jammed under his body (likely).
Bored (likely). Ding his bell, slide closet door, wind up clock, etc.

TALK TO HIM

*

Peggy says, "He's better 'cause he's got his fan on 'cause he's *tough*. He *likes* being tough." He does? "Yep."

July 28   Today when Emily went to feed Little John in his bed, abstractedly, she suddenly realized he was smiling and smiling at her, just because she was there! She had not spoken, so he must have seen her—unless he had heard, with very sharp ears. Tonight he is laughing and *silly* as I put him down to bed, and it quite takes away the memory of last night when we were up to him *eight or ten* times—even though by the time I am writing this down, he groans.

I step outside to the patio. The shapes of bushes are dimly but distinctly lighted from the lamps indoors, the stars seem to be heading down into the mountains, and the night sounds pick up, crickets throbbing in regular rhythms, like choruses, and then, far away, some birds. There is a wariness, snakes may be moving, and we have sniffed a skunk nearby. Light at night is like shadow in daytime, the lesser presence—and so are men.

In a three-page letter from Dr. Michaels: "Your gratitude continues to overwhelm me, and I can still only mumble a few meager protests to the fact that I had very little or nothing to do with it. Call it mystical or whatever you like— I just happened to be at a certain place at a certain time. Despite that you should know what a feeling of gratification I have gotten—one which I don't expect to be repeated in my medical career."

August 1 A bad night. But it's good that he seems to be differentiating his complaints: wet diaper, stiff bones, loneliness; and sometimes Weltschmerz?

August 5 This morning, before inserting the tube, I sat Little John up on his table, his back holding him surprisingly straight, his head requiring support. He laughed and laughed. Peggy came along, drawn by his laughter, and said, "John's sitting up!" with a great delight that was delightful to see.

August 6 As we went to bed last night, a terrible storm with Emily, who was full of despair about our life here. Everyone was so helpful in Colorado. Why did we ever come back? This

183   The Life of a Special Child

is, I suppose, the letdown after the euphoria of Little John's recovery. Finally, after acknowledging to her my own despair, I told her: We are throwing away the whole meaning of that recovery by giving ourselves up to this depression. That he recovered and is alive and as happy as he can be is a miracle nearly. We must keep our sense of joy in this miracle *active,* not letting ourselves despair over a bad afternoon and evening. Only this way can we draw out from his center the spokes and spirals of a little community—a group of those for whom his existence matters and who can take joy from his, and our, joy in his living. We must show that we aren't keeping John at home to indulge ourselves.

I read that the keeper of Tai-me, the sacred effigy of the Kiowa Indians, was supposed never to leave it after sundown. We cannot leave Little John after sundown. Are we the keepers of a Tai-me? Certainly of a sacred trust.

Talking with a local writer, groping to explain what we feel about Little John, Emily said that if you accept and understand children like this, you find in them a being as worthy as, and more pure than, in normal children. And he, "They become symbols of a level of meaning and existence we did not know about. All through literature, people like Little John have been used to express the inexpressible."

August 13   "The radiant beautiful smile". . . "feeling suspended out of time with him"—phrases from Emily talking on the phone— she is able to use such language, without affectation, because of what it simply describes.

We have noticed how nervously some new visitors can behave until they get to know Little John. Their eyes don't like settling on him—the tube in his nose, perhaps, whose purpose they misunderstand: "Is that to do with his breathing?" They edge around him and perch out of reach as if they were birds and he a cat. They avoid talking of him, let alone *to* him. We try to ease them along, help them understand that talking to him is not too different from talking to any five-year-old boy, or one-year-old, or whatever.

More than once, here in Southern California, we have been offered the reincarnation theory of Little John. Our neighbor—a kindly, cheery, typical grandmother from Iowa except that she is a studious Buddhist—said to Emily that of course he is paying for his sins in a previous existence. Emily was astonished and angered. Look at him, she wanted to say, on the contrary he must be a particularly holy being, an avatar, to be dealing so well with his afflictions. But she likes her, so she kept quiet.

This whole reading, though, is ridiculous and demeaning. Little John is *himself,* first and always, neither an inert receptacle nor a variation on anybody's else's theme, and he suffers or enjoys according to his restricted capacities to receive what passes inside his brain. But his *soul* is complete, individual, harmonious within its split directions like polyphonic music—no simple melody, this!—and indestructibly present. *It's a strange faith you lend us,* little fellow.

"Who are you writing to, Daddy?" asks Peggy, as I write this down.

"That's a good question," I tell her. "To Peggy for one."

August 27 Emily brings me an article in today's paper about a seven-year-old boy who had been six months in a coma after being hit by a car. Transferred to Orthopedic Hospital as a "hopeless case," he was put onto "maximum care"—everyone, including the cleaning people, was instructed to stop by his bed, *talk to him,* stroke him, move his limbs. Finally one day he said "Hi" to one of them. "It went all over the hospital," a nurse said, " 'Craig said *Hi!*' " And now he is up and out, and back for a checkup, laid out smiling on an examining table, in white underpants, the nurses and doctors smiling all around, and in another photo he is running, digging in down the corridor, grinning.

Emily did not see how my eyes were swelling. This was *our* blond thin naked boy in white diaper pants who had recovered from hopeless unconsciousness through attentive, maximum care. I told her. And she said: Last night she had had the thought that her being there, on that critical Sunday afternoon, stroking Little John's hand and talking to him softly, while he was still comatose, may have some-how been a turning point at which he stopped, and con-sidered about going away altogether, and decided no, there were good reasons not to.

Our need for a larger house was growing more pressing as the time for school drew near. As much as we loved the little foothill place we had made our own, and as fully as it had served us before our year in Colorado, it no longer would do. We could see that its distance from town would be-come steadily more inconvenient as the children grew—soon we would be driving Peggy four miles to nursery school—and their healthy boisterous-ness reverberated mercilessly down its hallway. To the confusion of re-settling, then, we added almost daily trips with a real estate agent to see what houses were for sale—each trip breaking into the day's more critical demands, and none of them turning up what we needed.

Part of what we needed was an extra room for a live-in helper. Our free-dom in Colorado had resulted largely from having that, and though we had had to adjust to several changes of personnel, the presence of a third adult in an emergency had been reassuring as well as liberating. Since returning to California, we had undergone a rapid turnover of temporary helpers, and for the year ahead we wanted more stability.

On the first of September, word reached us through a chain of friends of a huge house for rent on one of the nearby beaches. It had been left by a wealthy family to an order of nuns, who usually filled it with their teach-ing sisters. But this year they had decided not to wear their habits, and the Cardinal had forbidden them to teach without them; so the place would be available. They preferred a responsible family and would set the rent at something we could afford—in fact, at about what we had paid in Colorado for a smaller house.

We hesitated. The first day we saw it, it seemed gloomy, with dark old furniture and departed ecclesiastical presences. Each room was jammed with single beds like a dormitory. But two days later, in despair of finding anything more suitable, we took a second look. This time a flock of cheerful novices in shorts and sun tops was sweeping and dusting, washing the windows, and starting to pack away the extra beds. The sun was shining into a large glassed porch—perfect for wheeling Little John around in—and the beach was right at the door, wide and flat for the other children to play on. There were numerous rooms—enough for *two* live-in helpers if we wanted. And although the trains roared past right behind the garage, the surf's noise was steady and soothing. Why not? we thought, and arranged to take it in a couple of weeks.

September 1   Peggy is wheeling her French toast, cut up into little blocks, around the living room in her little red wheelbarrow. Andrew is puzzled.

The Sentimental Man holds Little John across his arms, dances to old Pete Seeger's "Freight Train"—no more dancing him on the shoulder because of the tube—and the feelings return—old music of populist dreams of the thirties, now fled, on a record we used to play in this house and room when Little John was three: "Freight train; freight train, going so fast."

September 5   Little John choking—the tube had worked loose and, as Emily was pouring the evening milk in, it was squirting into his nose. He fought like hell for his breath, and regained it himself, every muscle screwed up tight. I'm not sure what we could have done if he hadn't.

September 6   How Little John *changes*. He is immensely more aware and

187   The Life of a Special Child

discriminating than when we first came home. He knows our voices well and responds differently to John and me, and also to Peggy and Andrew. He laughs when Andrew cries but is very upset if Peggy does—perhaps it sounds to him more like his own crying. He is more touchy, often sad, and can be furiously angry. When he is really mad, he cries so loudly it hurts our ears. Usually this seems to be from intestinal pains.

Tonight, though, he cried apparently in rage, going quiet whenever I sat with my hands on him, rocking him, but starting up if I left, like any child not wanting to go to bed. Finally we sedated him. We feel such a strong sense of his inability to tell us why he is crying—his tummy, his head, or pain in his heart? But I don't feel the hopeless grief at it that I did when he was younger.

September 11   Woke Peggy and reminded her she was going to nursery school today. She talked nonstop about it for the next hour—such mental vigor and excitement! Told us all the things she would do with "Mrs. Garbund," and as John took her off, she called back comfortingly, "I'll be back later, Mummy."

When I went to pick her up, her teacher had already talked to Dr. Riordan. "You have a most interesting situation at home," she told me. I said I thought it had made Peggy more mature. "Oh *yes,* she's amazing. We have had others with handicapped siblings who have been very disturbed. She went up to a little boy who was crying and tried to comfort him." I said that is what she does at home for Little John. "You should be very proud of her."

"We are."

As we were driving home, Peggy looked up in the sky and declared, "The moon has come back from his friend the dark."

September 16   Phoned the university's job placement and housing offices to advertise for a student helper, trying to explain what we need—a special sort of girl, lively, inventive (as one of those we had this summer, though a splendid housekeeper and busy as a beaver, was not), dependable, cheerful. Five minutes later, a call from a girl, Claudia, who had been sitting at the desk when the phone rang. She drove right out. We showed her Little John, who was lying happily on the carpet, played with him a little, and then we took her down to the big beach house. "It's got real wood, real windows," she exclaimed—in contrast to the jerry-built student apartments she is used to. "Oh, I'll work so hard!" She seemed nice, and we decided to try it out; in two weeks she will move in. Later in the day, a phone call from a girl at the other office. Suggested she come talk to us tomorrow. After all, since there will be two rooms, why not two girls to share the load?

*

In my mail at the university, the nursing school paper by Denise Scovill on caring for Little John, for which she received an A+. It is clear and informative and accurate, and in sections, especially "psychological aspects," very touching and interesting. "My first feeling about the child was that of fear," she admits. "I do not know why I react with fear to certain deformities or illnesses initially, but it was as usual very brief, and when I began to take part in his physical care, I found him enjoyable and fun to work with."

September 17   The second girl, Jami, phoned to say she had changed her mind and would not come. I could not pin down her reason—too far to drive, too expensive for gas, she said. I said, if this was her *real* reason, perhaps we could help her pay

189   The Life of a Special Child

for the gas. Why didn't she come and meet us, and if it wasn't the real reason, please tell us. She came out and saw Little John and seemed gentle with him. She has worked with handicapped children and is studying speech therapy. She too became enthusiastic about the beach house and in the end decided she would like to stay with us. She can move in as soon as we want. Will she and Claudia do? Will they get on together? No way to tell but trying them out.

September 18   As we prepare to leave this house, ours for only four years but the first we have owned and one we have deeply loved and changed, what we feel is *gratitude,* not nostalgia. It has given us what we needed, a quiet place for Little John's noisy and painful years, and for Peggy's and Andrew's beginnings. Now we're too many for it, and it retaliates by clashing our commotions back on our ears—we feel like Little John when the world is too loud and he cries.
Dreams
1. "He has died." Emily was speaking to me, having gone in to Little John.
2. I was a parent assisting in a small school for retarded children. Little John was one of the children. I saw him either throw or catch a ball. I realized I would not be a very good assistant because I would give too much attention to my own child.

September 22.   The night of the move, exhausted, all our mover friends
At the beach.   faded away, a hot dinner left for us by another friend, we sat alone at the big formal dining table beneath the elaborate chandeliers and gazed out across the vast Oriental carpets, down the enormous living room, dimly lighted, and felt like interlopers—far too much grandeur and majesty for folks like us! It seems more homelike with Jami here

190   And Say What He Is

now, who is very sweet and has worked all day long each day to help us get settled. Although we are tired, it is refreshing to be able to walk out the door onto the beach.

There is a wide, warm porch, roofed with translucent plastic, which the sea breeze blows into, and lots of space there and all through the house for rolling Little John around in his stroller. He sleeps in the large room that opens off ours and fronts on the ocean. A big plate glass window facing south to receive the full sun; we have set his changing table under it. His chimes hang by the crib, in the farthest seaward corner, and since there is a huge radio-TV-phonograph in the living room, we have put our small stereo set in here for him. We feel a comfort to have him so near us when we sleep. But he is, still, a sick boy, and this is, a little, a hospital. We are always on call.

September 25   Mani was driven up to see us by a kind friend. She was staying with some very rich people, and beside them she showed a lack of self-confidence that I had never dreamed existed. She was almost relegated to the role of country mouse or poor relation. Not quite, though, for the Presbyterian Scot is a proud breed, and she was the daughter of an aristocrat. So when one of them had given her a rapid rundown on her children's whereabouts, and then said rudely, "You got all that now?" Mani retorted gamely, "I've got the one in Bangkok, and I'll try to have the others straight by the morning."

We find ourselves more able to appreciate her generosity— that she *would* drag herself all this way to see us and spend a long afternoon and evening with us and the children, keeping alert to all we said and did—enjoying Andrew's fatness and coy smile, following Peggy with a quick eye and tongue, and seeing and sensing Little John's beauty as strongly as anyone ever has. "He's such a handsome wee fellow," she

191   The Life of a Special Child

said, "so brave." The rift caused by our earlier fierce disagreements about him has narrowed and closed as she has come to appreciate better what he really is. However, she still harbors some unrealistic idea that his "intellect" is really all right, if only he had not been hampered by "this other thing."

September 26   If Little John's life is a model of human life, and it is, it proves that our aim is always for happiness, which existence—time—impedes. Each happy day or moment is an achievement of the mind against these impediments. To be human is to *see,* to achieve action against accident, and to recover. But the contrary is also true. To be human is to accept limitations, to be blind, to move and roll with the accidents of existence, rather than wrestling vainly against them. Life goes on in the swirls of experience around these two poles, not on any straight line between them.

October 8   Rosalie comes to tea, bringing Frannie, who originally introduced *her* to our family—two of Little John's oldest friends! We all have a fine time on the sun porch, John in his stroller, happy to hear Rosalie's voice—he seems to recognize her. Or is it that she has precisely the right way of talking to him? Then he laughs hilariously while she pushes him around all through the house in his stroller.

October 10   We are thoroughly settled. The two girls have arranged their class schedules so that one of them is always here, and Alice comes on Saturdays to give them a day off. They both work hard and cheerfully, dragging buckets of diapers to the wash, tidying and cleaning, giving themselves completely.

We are going through a rough time with Peggy—sassy, independent, cheeky, pushy—new habits, it seems, from nursery school. Whenever we have any minor crisis with

192   And Say What He Is

Little John, she complains, "I don't feel very well." She feels squeezed between the two boys, I think, though, goodness knows, she does most of the squeezing!

October 11 Emily phones me at school. Little John has the family cold, temperature 101°. Immediate worry, though no longer (since the summer) sheer panic. I don't need to *race* home.

Later, he is responding to the medicine. He has a quiet evening, but at eleven he is still awake, though quiet. At his last feeding he went through a series of seizurelike flutterings and shudders, his hands drawn up to his shoulders with fingers spread and bent, like talons.

October 12 When was it—the other night?—that Little John was giving us so much trouble, crying, keening? Then there were some relatively easy days. Now tonight with his cold he is giving out loud, voiced groans, higher-pitched complaints, which drag at us and drag us apart, one from the other.

"As if he's *fighting* the drug," says Emily, "as if he knows what it is."

October 14 A peaceful morning, Peggy and Big John at school. I have the cold, so I sit in Little John's room, which is drenched with sunlight reflecting off the water, talking to Little John and to Andrew, who is tripping in and out of the room on tippy-toes, running, stuffs a sock in my hand, wraps my fingers around the gift, bounces up on the couch, runs away and back, unlike Peggy, who used to move mainly in order to explore and always with caution. Little John, within his limits, was more like Andrew, delighting in movement for its own sake and reckless about it.

In the night, a long spell up and down to Little John. It reminds us what a strange little boy he is—what a sick little boy. "And what a strange life we lead," John adds.

October 20	I was laid flat with an attack of vomiting, which seems to result from being overtired. Peggy was unusually gentle all day, helping Andrew with his toys until I revived. When he came to see me for the first time, a coy smile—I have a secret I'm not telling, but maybe I love my mother—and I responded warmly. He's so beautiful now, with his thick yellow hair and big eyes. Peggy advanced menacingly on him to grab away a toy. He looked at her with mingled fear and anger, and as she pushed him, for the first time he resisted and shoved her back three steps. She was outraged at his presumption!
October 21	Little John's great sweetness tonight and yesterday evening, when he smiled and gave his indrawn laugh on hearing a couple of noisy, driving old Beatles records that we hadn't played for a long time.
October 22	Jami confided that she and Claudia had discovered each was afraid the other was working harder and so an unspoken competition was developing as to who could do the most for us. Also that they had been too timid to eat breakfast with us or to have second helpings at dinner! I think John broke the ice the first time he said something silly at the table, realized he had done so, and laughed at himself; they realized that even professors are human. Jami admitted too that the real reason for her original hesitancy about coming out for an interview—which had seemed evasive and had worried me—was that she thought we were a rich family looking for a cheap maid. At any rate, everything is much more comfortable now—a huge household, but it runs smoothly, and there's so much attention and love for all three children.
Monday, October 28	We were having dinner at Lou and Tim's on Saturday

194   And Say What He Is

night, when a call came, at 10:30, from Jami—not about Little John, but Andrew, who was coughing and having difficulty breathing. I told her to phone the doctor while we raced home. It turned out to be the croup, Andrew barking like a seal and feeling very sad. Dr. Shelton, of former acquaintance, was on call and had told Jami to take Andrew to Emergency right away. She explained that she couldn't leave the other two. "If the parents are not home in five minutes, you will *have* to come. Make some arrangement for the other children." She was panicked, with nobody to turn to. When we got home, we rushed Andrew in to Emergency, and then we had to wait twenty minutes for the damned doctor to show up. The nurses were quite calm, and charmed with Andrew, while his breathing rasped and echoed from the steel equipment around the big rooms. They gave him shots, admitted him to Pediatrics, and put him in an oxygen tent, where we saw him relieved, and off to sleep.

The next morning he was sitting up, squeezing a squeaky toy, drops of water running down off limp strands of hair over his face, looking damply adorable in his plastic house. He stayed a second night, the girls taking turns to be by him all day, and I picked him up today, by which time he had become so lively that they had him tethered by one foot to stop him bouncing out of the crib. "Are we glad to see *you!*" said the nurse. Dr. Riordan says if it happens again he will treat him at home.

October 30   Little John has another cold, and Dr. Riordan came over during his lunch hour to give him the shot. Closer to town, I feel we can accept his generosity, whereas we were just too far away for him to visit at our old house. He says he will always come at any hour for Little John; no need for us to bring him to the office, which would be a considerable effort and add some risk of exposing him to other germs. He has *never sent us a bill* for treating Little John.

Tonight he came to dinner. Told us to be more "aggressive" about feeding Little John, taking him *to* experiences, sitting him up. He even seems to think he would be able to eat by mouth again. I don't.

November 5   A beautiful day, the ocean calm, the air warm, the children running on the beach at low tide against the blue and gold light—Andrew never stopping, running on his toes, his little fair head bobbing, Peggy and the girl next door digging in the sand, their two dark heads together. Little John lay content in the blaze of sun, smiling as the little breezes blew over him. The sea was like a golden silk spread.

December 6   Looking at early pictures of Little John—how faint, frail, delicate his happiness. His limp hands. His stare: direct to the lens, or away, across camera, not solemn but as if listening to a hidden message telling him, *All will not be right; yet be not troubled, for all will be well (and all manner of things will be well),* and he receives the message and is satisfied. A message we were not yet able to hear, but it was caught in the photographs, in the shapes of light and shadow. I look at them now, not able to bear it yet.

December 10   A friend phones, a poet. He thinks Little John might be cured through some miraculous medical discovery. Cured to what? The damage has been done. Nothing more fatuous to think about.

*

Jami has observed Peggy playing a private game—if seen, she has a smile of "Now you've caught me." The fingers of her hand are people, which the other hand points to: Dr. Riordan, Rosalie, Mummy, Peggy, and Andrew. "No, you aren't Peggy," she will say to her fourth finger, "Peggy is bigger. Peggy is this one" (her middle finger). "And then here's tiny little Dr. Riordan" (her thumb!).

The fall had passed in alternating illness and health for us all, with numerous visitors, and always busy. Before Christmas, tiny little Dr. Riordan urged us to take a break—we had had none since the spring vacation in Colorado, and it had been a heavy, strenuous year. Get away, and don't think about Little John for a week, he told us—leave him in the hospital, and we'll take care of him. Our memories of John's miraculous happiness at Children's Hospital were still vivid, and we had in mind also Riordan's recent advice to be more adventurous, and so we accepted. On the night of December 12 we took Little John into the hospital with nothing wrong with him, for once. We wrote out long lists of instructions about his medicines and routines and were satisfied that the staff would do its best to follow them. Jami and Claudia would be visiting him once or twice a day, while Rosalie, a nurses' aide now, was working on the floor below and would visit him in her free time and wheel him around the ward in his stroller. It seemed a safe and comfortable haven, better than leaving him at home since the girls would have their hands full there with Peggy and Andrew. With sufficient confidence we headed back once more to the Indian country of northern Arizona and New Mexico.

December 13   Last night I phoned Jami, who said they had taken the tube out; would I call the hospital? Much anxiety. When I reached them, I found Riordan had ordered it—he wants them to try feeding Little John by mouth; he still thinks we aren't being adventurous enough. They assured me they could handle it. I hope so. When we crossed the border into Arizona, I felt acutely distressed. We need a break, but should we be going so far?

December 15	Jami reports all is well. Little John was *not* able to take food by mouth, so now the tube stays in, as we had directed. The hour before phoning these last three nights I have been frantic with anxiety, a sense that something catastrophic must have happened while we are driving to a phone booth farther and farther from home. Each time, everything has been all right. Peggy and Andrew are very excited to talk to us on the phone. "I love you very much. Are you coming home now?" Peggy has made herself a favored visitor in the ward. A boy about her age was screaming away, and nobody had been able to soothe him. Then they became aware he had stopped, looked over, and she was standing talking to him. "I said, 'Jonathan, why are you crying?' and he didn't say anything," she reported to us. The nurses say she can come in there whenever she wants.

December 21	Home again, after ending our trip with two lovely snowy days in Santa Fe, which made the whole journey seem worthwhile. The loveliest thing we saw was the snow falling gently on the old painted wooden Santos figures around the crèche in the open patio of La Fonda Hotel. We raced a blizzard out of Flagstaff and, after stopping last night, drove home across the California desert, shimmering with snow instead of its usual moondust. Jami and Claudia and the children were all very excited to see us. "They haven't taken very good care of Little John," Jami warned us; "you will be glad to get him home."

When we went in to the hospital, I was startled by his look, his eyes staring wildly, rolling constantly in frantic nystagmus, and his face so strange. Yes, he *does* look abnormal, I thought; we must be fooling ourselves, he's very strange-looking. While we were gathering his things together, Gina, one of the nurses Jami had gotten to know, apologized, "We didn't have time to look after him properly." She said that lots of nurses had been out with the flu, and everyone brings in the children during the holidays for tonsillectomies. We came home sobered.

Jami and Claudia tell us that he didn't get his meals on time, didn't get the fussing and soothing that he is used to. The noises of other kids had upset him, and also the constant crackle of the TV sets, slung from the ceiling like bomb racks. Already, tonight, by bedtime he was smiling at our voices, the contours of his face had changed, and he looked more like himself, though his eyes were still wild.

*

The longest night of the year, and it was. We rediscover why we had to take a vacation. Andrew up and out to us all night, countless times; Emily up to Little John three times. We know, as we already realized on the trip, that we could never leave him in hospital while we went to visit her family in New Zealand.

December 22 Sunday—Sun Day. Little John kept getting happier all morning as we sat in his room and laughed and made up silly songs:

He's as chipper as a kipper with a flipper,
He's as chipper as a kipper in the sea,
He's as chipper as a kipper
And as bold as Jack the Ripper,
Eating kipper with a cup of toast and tea!

He was himself again, all smiles, all patient joy, his eyes normal. "His eyes are so soft," said Jami. "In the hospital they got so *strange.*"

199   The Life of a Special Child

December 24   Jami tells us, "John is so *happy.*"

We ask, "You mean different from the way he was in hospital?"

"Oh yes"—and she tells us more.

For the first three days, in spite of their taking the tube out and having trouble replacing it, he was relatively himself. He would respond immediately when Jami or Claudia arrived to talk to him. Later in the week he began to look sad, and as each day went by, he became more blank-looking and would take longer to smile at them. Then when they brought him back from a walk in the stroller and lifted him onto the bed, he would start screaming because he knew they were leaving him. "Please don't ever leave him in hospital again," Jami pleaded. "Leave him with us, we'll take care of him." She would have told us Little John was unhappy, on our phone calls, but Dr. Riordan told her not to, since there was no actual danger, and he thought we needed the vacation.

We are all amazed that Little John should come back to himself, and to us, so quickly. He has been not so much ecstatic—as he was in Colorado at returning from the shadows—as deeply, contentedly happy. He is smiling and cracking up over the newest Beatles records, and is soothed by our lullabies when he is distraught in the night, and he smiles, all comforted, when changed, after shrieking with wet diapers. How can one but marvel at all this joy and gentleness, just because we are nice to him?

"He's just so *good!*" says Jami. "He's so happy to be home that he is being good so you won't punish him by putting him back in hospital!"

Christmas Day   A somewhat hurly-burly Christmas, lots of excitement, all of us pleased with our presents. Peggy offering her toys to Andrew, but at the end taking over *all his* as well as her own. Little John very happy with new records and a parrot mobile. Jami, the dear girl, thanked me for the day, "It meant so much," and when I hugged her and thanked her, there were tears in her eyes. How could we do other than make her one of us, when she is giving up all her vacation to help us?

December 27 Tonight, holding Little John after taking his tube out, I noticed he was deliberately closing his mouth, apparently for the sheer feel of it. Also he was looking at the spinning bright music box with his eyes open and steady, not wavering. All this implies more conscious control than we have been crediting him with—a growing, or a growing-back? He continues very contented, happy all day.

December 30 [From a letter to the grandfather]
Little John is like an angel, sweet, responsive, delighted at any attention. Just one week in hospital showed us how he would drift away from us if left in an institution. The level of his awareness and responses depends utterly on the love he receives. He basks in tenderness and being cherished— as indeed we all do—but Little John's whole life is dependent on it. I think we realize this the more, too, for seeing the transformation in one night, as he understood he was back with us safely again. Such total appreciation is a little miracle—which is what Little John is.

1969

January 1   We walk into the new year, along the beach after midnight. The ocean slips very small wavelets at us, the new sand very strangely wide and flat offers to be written on with our foot tracks. We write our resolution on it in boots. We know now that we have no way of knowing what the year will bring to us and Little John. The pattern of our lives is full, and within the pattern, including Little John's disorders, rests the meaning.

January 8   Emily phones me at school: Little John's cold is no better; he is very sleepy and dopey, has a fever of 102°; will I hurry home? He seems to be breathing more freely—responds to our talk. But his temperature, an hour later, has gone up to 104°. We rush him to Dr. Riordan, thinking it may be pneumonia again (but believing he can shake it). And it isn't! He has "cold sores"—what used to be called trench mouth—inflamed and bleeding rings around his teeth. He is given a shot, which really hurts and angers him. Through the rest of the day he improves. Tonight he is happy and calm, though his eyes are a little staring.

January 13   Little John lethargic and full of phlegm from his cold. Dr. Riordan comes to the house. "What you need is a course in nursing." Need to keep the airway clear. "He can't breathe through all that mucous, and his muscles are weak anyway." We can rent a suction machine. And, referring to his time in the hospital before Christmas, "He wouldn't survive if you left him with people who didn't love him."

     He talked too about adoptions—they should be public affairs, announced in the paper like marriages and divorces and births. Anyone who wants to should be able to adopt —single women, single men, anyone—and they should be able to adopt any kind of kid, autistic, retarded, handicapped, whatever—no limits. Some adopters are too nervous; they don't want to do anything wrong.

"You don't need to give me Christmas presents. Knowing Little John is enough. You only meet people like him a few times in your life."

January 15   Jami's father came by to see her, and she took him in to meet Little John. He went in shyly, but without embarrassment he said, "Why, he's a lovely little fellow, a nice little guy!" Little John beamed at the warmth in his voice, and then Jami's father was delighted, "Why he's smiling at me, the sweet little guy," and Little John smiled even more. It was a beautiful moment. *Recognition* seems to be at the root of it—Little John recognizing true feeling in a voice, and the other person recognizing the person in Little John.

January 21   Peggy talking: "Is John sick or not?" No. "So we don't need to take his tempachoo?"

January 31   [From a letter to the grandfather]
In haste I wanted to let you know we are all right, since you may have heard the news about the flood. We *were* in it, but we are safe, and nearly resettled, though exhausted. Before dawn last Saturday John was wakened by a muffled thump, which was the front corner of our seawall going out, pushed by a huge force of water that had been running with incredible speed for several days beside the house in an old concrete channel. The water immediately began to undercut the farthest corner of Little John's room; we had moved his crib back from there to the inner wall a few days before as a precaution when the rains were particularly

203   The Life of a Special Child

heavy. So we lifted him into his stroller and rushed him through to the other side of the house away from the water. Then I woke the girls while John was discovering the only road out was blocked by mud and flowing water, and when a call to the Fire Department for help produced none—all their units were out—and a warning of higher water on the way, we decided to leave at once in case the entire channel wall collapsed behind the house and cut us off. We gathered up the sleeping children, and as we wrapped them each in a Navaho blanket to keep them dry, we heard muffled crashes as more of the wall gave way. We walked out to the railroad tracks, which are on higher ground behind the house, each of the others carrying a child, and I carrying a box of Little John's medicines, tubes, and Sustagen. Then we made our escape by stepping along the crossties, over the trestle bridge with the flood waters raging underneath. As Jamie said later, "There we were, with only the clothes we wore, thinking we would never see any of our possessions again, each holding a child in an Indian blanket, and it was *enough*."

We took shelter in a hotel with cottages farther down the line. I got a key to a cottage and fed the children with milk and cereal, which the hotel people very ungraciously supplied ("But who is going to *pay* for it?"), and then hurried back along the tracks with a bevy of nuns from the house across the stream (one of their bedrooms, vacated only twenty minutes before, had already washed away without a trace) to collect dry diapers, baby clothes, toys, anything we could quickly gather from the solid side of the house. The children were unafraid and curious—they had been asleep when we were all so frightened—because Jami and Claudia stayed with them and created an island of calm. As the day went by, various friends arrived after fording streams and made dashes into the doomed bedrooms, now

entirely undercut, to carry out armloads of goods. We
handed boxes of our things to complete strangers who were
sight-seeing along the tracks, so that at one time I looked
back on a three-hundred-yard line of people staggering
along under our burdens. One of these women went home
and prepared a hot meal for us and brought it by. There
was mounting chaos in the little two-bedroom cottage as
the boxes flowed in and with them the mud on everybody's boots.

The next morning, having heard more heavy downpours
in the night, we rushed along to see what had happened to
the house. The two outer bedrooms, ours and Little John's,
had collapsed and fallen into the creek, now somewhat
subsided. Surprisingly, the rest of the house was intact. We
crept in cautiously and looked through what had been our
bedroom door—the roar of water was now *inside* the bedroom, books were floating in the far corner where Little
John's crib had been, everywhere there were broken boards,
tiles fallen in from the roof, chips of plaster, the floor-
boards hanging almost vertically. The desolation and sense
of doom made us frantic to remove *everything* still left in
the whole house, and so for the second day a stream of
friends, passersby, and students of John's slaved to salvage
things from the shattered rooms and carry out all we pos-
sessed—by car now, as the road out was clear—to attics and
garages all over town.

Since then we have been house hunting. After four days
of endless phone calls and exhausting forays out to see
every possible and impossible house in the city, we are
buying a slightly rundown but lovely old Spanish-style place
from a family about to leave for Africa—they signed the
papers this afternoon an hour before boarding the train! We
will be right in town, with lots of rooms—we couldn't think
of parting with the girls now that we have been through so

much with them—and a big garden, well away from the ocean or any stream!

Little John seems none the worse, though he was a bit upset the day of the flood. But keeping him calm and comfortable added an extra edge of urgency to everything we did. I won't write more now. We have been running so hard we feel breathless, and we want to rest quietly for a day or two before we move in on Tuesday, when the sale, hastened along by our incredibly kind realtor friend, will close, and the house will be ours. The girls have been so calm, so responsible, and so selfless, working so hard for us, and all of us need a little quiet.

Tuesday, February 4

We move onto the hill, into a fifty-year-old white stucco house with a red tile roof. It is built on terraces, which extend into the garden, all scrambling up the hillside like a Tibetan city; many tall trees, bushes, three plots of strawberry plants, and, grotesquely, smack underneath a set of climbing poles, a small grave marker, "Our little dog Topper went to sleep," with a date in 1958. Inside, there are corner fireplaces and tall narrow French doors opening onto tiny balconies that look down on a fountain with scalloped basins and a pool. We are lucky to be in it.

And what of Little John? He is happy here. I carry him around the house, down the narrow shadowed hall, out into the bright living room, around the corner into his own small light room, down a step into the tile-floored dining room, out onto the open brick patio, and he *smiles*. "Oh, he does like this house!" Emily exclaims.

February 5

Boxes everywhere, coming back from garages all over town, packed by rescuers, carted off until we had a house to put them in, and now here they are, and I have no idea what's in them. But we are managing—the essentials were put away

206   And Say What He Is

in cupboards yesterday by good friends so the household could keep running. And today some of John's students are still lugging things in and helping unpack, with a cheeriness and clowning in great contrast to the anxiety of evacuating the other house. It's sunny and there's lots of laughter. What a lot of good friends we have, dozens of people have worked their hearts out for us. All we can feel is thankful—to the fates for not being more cruel than they were, to all these good people toiling in and out of both houses to rescue us and to help us move in.

February 13   Jami and Claudia tell us they don't think of Little John as "retarded" or "handicapped" or any such category—only as "Little John." They have become aware of this when other people say, "Oh, the poor thing, he's so terribly handicapped." "No," they answer, "that's just Little John. *He's* not 'handicapped'—that's just the way he is." We were very moved. This is the whole story, and they've come to it themselves.

February 18   Little John very angry with a cold tonight. Emily phones and is given a runaround from Dr. Riordan's answering service; she retorts, "Well *I'm* sorry, but Dr. Riordan has instructed *me* to always try to reach *him* first." In three minutes he is phoning back. She and Claudia manage to get a teaspoon of Hycodan cough syrup down his throat without choking him. He is furious, and they are delighted, amazed that he could swallow it. Had not wanted the fuss of putting the tube in for just one teaspoonful of medicine.

February 19   Fiercely, as we are trying to go to bed, John screams, very angry, coughs, chokes, splutters, afraid of not being able to breathe. Will we have to take turns sleeping and watching? This evening we saw a movie of World War II in Paris. In

207   The Life of a Special Child

one scene, as the family waited in a shelter for the all-clear, I thought how impossible it would be to keep Little John alive under such conditions. In fact, of course, there are many situations even today where it would be out of the question to sustain him. We are lucky in having the money to afford a house big enough to include two girls to help with him. (There would be ways of managing to keep him with less money, but not easily.) What does this mean? That he is lucky, as well as we?

When you can't reach him
the wires all burned out
nothing plugged in
works   flip the switch
nothing

*

Little John in a panic, unable to sleep due to the difficulty of breathing through his mucous. I was afraid to sedate him with Seconal because it depresses the breathing. He would try to gasp air through his mouth, relax, almost fall asleep, then startle, draw a nose breath, find it blocked, and panic, struggling with great, snorting, chest-heaving efforts to pull the air through his nostrils. His fingernails looked a bit blue from lack of oxygen, so Dr. Riordan felt he should go into the hospital, and drove him down himself, with John holding him. After they left I felt very low, sure he would not return, the Denver crisis beginning again.

February 20   1:17 A.M. by the clock on the wall of the hospital. I carried John straight in, up the elevator to Pediatrics. The head nurse had a bed all ready and in an instant had suctioned his throat and nostrils completely clear with the machine.

Now Dr. Riordan is giving her full instructions. She jabs John with a shot of relaxant in his bottom. He is so mad he can scarcely find his voice to scream—outraged! But in ten minutes he *has* relaxed and is breathing much more calmly. I can go home and reassure Emily that he is on the mend.

*

Morning   Little John looked fine, nose clear (though nostrils blood-stained from suctioning) and color better. He wasn't very happy though. I stayed with him most of the day. Gina, the nurse who apologized for their care of him during Christmas vacation, came down, although it was her day off, and spent several hours there to relieve me. She will be leaving her present apartment soon and will move into our empty spare room.

February 22   Brought Little John home from hospital this morning. Time to get him away from the impersonality there. He was fading off.

February 24   Bought a nice Danish sofa bed to set by the living room windows as a daybed for Little John. The sun comes in on him there, and he can listen to records, to the cars going up the road, to the soft sounds of water dripping in the fountain, as he does in his own room, but closer to the rest of the household. He has seemed happier in the living and dining rooms than stuck away in his bedroom.

The children from next door are so friendly, playing well with Peggy and Andrew, all out on the lawn yelling and laughing. Little John likes it too. We have to be careful, though, as he seems to sunburn more easily here; perhaps it is the lack of filtered shade, though he did not seem to

209   The Life of a Special Child

burn at the beach even in the full sun.

March 1   A Flood Party, to thank all our rescuers and helpers. All
told there were seventy people—neighbors, professors,
realtors, the piano mover who loaded and stored all our
large furniture, the bunch of students who are always
around now, doing odd jobs. It was a marvelous crowd,
cheerful, spilling out of the house onto the patio, eating
two hams and a turkey and dozens of loaves of fresh
French bread. The house has been well and truly *warmed*.

March 4   Enormous windstorm in the night. Huge cypress tree next
door blown down across the power lines.

March 6   Emily up to John, gave him Seconal.
1:00 A.M.
4:00 A.M.   Little John having difficulty breathing. Would breathe
twelve (or five or three) breaths, then hold his breath.
Mucous in sinuses? Woke Gina, the nurse, now living in the
spare room upstairs, and she gave a shot of antibiotic that
Dr. Riordan had sent home with her yesterday for just such
an emergency. It seemed to help right away. Turned on the
cool air vaporizer, and he was comfortable, so we managed
three hours' more sleep.

March 12   JOHN'S SIXTH BIRTHDAY!
Twice, before rising early, I dreamed of being in a house
two stories high, by a road that had been turned by floods
into a wide stream. The water seemed to be safely on the
far side away from the house, when a sudden surge drove
it toward us. It was welling around the house, and we had
to get out. (It was of course like our situation in January,
but the landscape was much larger, and there was no ocean.)
Emily was there, and Little John whom I carried. The
second time I dreamed it, the water was deeper, and the

house collapsed. I was holding Little John and a suitcase containing his medicines and tubes, and I had to duck us under the water. After my feet touched bottom, I found he was breathing OK, and I was merely cross. The strangest detail was that he seemed no larger than a newborn infant, yet with his present face.

SUN AND SHADOW

(for Little John's sixth birthday)

as we meet our own words
returning to us put into the mail
by another hand   how strangely

they walk to us   like a child
in a dream   walking
who could never walk out of the dream

the rhyme sounds return on themselves
and the beat that keeps beating
beats its meaning into the floor   the sun

which keeps ducking in and out
of the March sky   a croquet ball
tapped by a wooden mallet

brightens the days meanings with a clack
and then falls the long shadow
slowly as a rain rooted tree   silent

among us   if the light could only
hold and not fade   if we could float
weightless and always in sunlight

or in and out of the unhappy times
like chickadees splashing in a three-tiered fountain
or sparrows in a tall Italian cypress

Little John cross with his cold, not really *in it* for his birthday. Rosalie came to dinner, gave him a hurdy-gurdy musical bunny. Jami and Claudia presented him with some gaudy art nouveau pillow slips. Alice came by with a pair of chartreuse socks. Bill and Lisa phoned and asked if they could drop by, since they had shared his party last year in Colorado, and they stayed for the cake.

March 17 Some lovely weather, warm days, Little John out in the sun, and a flow of people in and around the house that is very pleasant. We have taken up a new life, as satisfying in its rhythms as our life in the beach house. And our family is much closer after what we went through.

March 18 Maybe Little John's presence slows down time. I don't feel Peggy's or Andrew's babyhood flying past as I would expect it to.

With Little John, each of us must give up a little of what his own ego would desire to have. Not too much, if the duty is divided and shared more or less evenly. If it were not divided evenly, those giving up most would resent those who gave less. Still, Emily has far more to do than I.

March 19 Little John is waking at night, often two or three times. Very hard to get him to sleep at eight; he seems to fight the Noctec. We may spend as much as an hour soothing him.

March 20 John and I go up the coast for two days, after a week of broken nights. There is a need to restore our awareness of each other.

March 21 The girls were up to Little John *eight* times last night, they report when we phone. We slept deeply. Here, only a couple of hours from home, we don't feel the anxiety we did at Christmas in Santa Fe, two days away. A thorough rest.

Monday, March 31

A dreadful, nerve-splitting day. Little John totally mashed the inside of his cheek with his teeth. He was crying and not attended to immediately—Jami and Claudia both away for spring vacation, and we were busy with electricians trying to discover the source of a power leak that is sending enough electricity under the dining room floor to *heat the tiles*. By the time we got to him, John had gone into paroxysms of screaming, completely rigid with his legs thrust out straight. Blood everywhere, in his bed.

He was so desperate that Emily hardly left him all day, sat holding a small cloth between his teeth and his cheek, soothing and rocking him. The cloth pulled three of his old teeth loose, little worn-down nubs. Tartar wiped off one easily. Blood and screams, curdling.

Tuesday, April 1

Today much like yesterday, the same paroxysms though less often. I felt that if we held the cloth and kept him from biting, his cheek might heal in 48 hours. Alice did wonderfully with the other two, and is staying overnight.

Wednesday, April 2

Claudia returned, and Alice went home. She commented that it was much more interesting to be living here than coming only on Saturday mornings; she could see all the parts of the day, and how the things that need to be done evolve out of the day before and out of the earlier duties. Little John calmer today, but we are nervous.

Thursday, April 3

Maundy Thursday. A colleague to dinner, full of Easter joy, a fortunate believer. Little John in considerable pain again.

213   The Life of a Special Child

Saturday, April 5 End of a terrible week—Little John fairly peaceful today, only bad when he had either anxiety or pain before a bowel movement. Some of his screaming must be from his constipation, though it is hard to believe that this alone could cause so much distress. What can we do for him when he is obviously in real anguish? Don't want to addict him to codeine, which works best.

So often we think the fabric of our lives just temporary threads, colors, patterns, but one day we will wake up to find these were our life itself, inextricable, intrinsic. Without them, not only the pattern gone, the fabric gone too, death. We are not two people waiting until the children grow up and leave, but changed, woven, shaped, sculpted by these children, these stresses, these forces, until they become *us*—we are no longer *ourselves* in any secret isolated sense. We are both loss and gain, joy and irritation, practical details and despair, playmates and nursemaids and nurses of children, desperate and relieved, wrought up or released from strain, fearful, anxious, snatching pleasure when we may, quiet when it passes elusively by.

April 6, Easter Sunday! Peggy and Andrew started dancing beside Little John's daybed, and in and out the doors to the porch in the sunlight, spinning and bouncing like his old Spin Twins, to Bach's Easter Oratorio. The fountain and the trees danced, and Little John smiled and laughed.

April 10 Little John on his mat on the dining room floor, in the warm morning sunlight, which soothes him after we have inserted the tube. I realized suddenly, and remarked to John, that although Andrew has tripped and fallen down on every square inch of floor in this house, he has never once fallen on Little John. It is from an awareness deeper than anything *we* could teach him.

April 15   After being quiet all yesterday, one leg purple halfway up and his cheeks puffy and flushed, there is a great improvement in Little John overnight; he wakes up happy and alert, and even his *feet* are hardly purplish. Emily recognized the signs of edema from last year in Boulder and knew what to do. He must have been accumulating too much sedative, so she gave him only a half-strength sleeping pill, and yet he slept through the night. We recognize again that there is never a fixed, permanent pattern, and the shifting keeps our responses alert. He stayed happy, and we all had a happy day.

*

Rocking Little John asleep in the night. He wakes up screaming, thrusting his legs down and arching his back. We place our hands along his ribs, over the narrow rim of his chest, hollowing our palms to cup it like a bony saddle—or warming them as on a coffee mug. Then we rock him from side to side, often quite vigorously, to shake the anger out of him. He relaxes, his breath starts coming smoothly, but then the arms push down and knock our hands aside, the legs jut out stiffly, and we must start over. The mind drifts, our eyes unfocus in the dim room, and we lose track of time, forget what we are doing, dreaming our hopes and fears for the future—when this treatment will no longer soothe him, what then?—until the steady pushing and pulling with the arms has joined the rhythms of his breathing. Startled, we come to ourselves. He is asleep.

April 20   Off for a Sunday brunch, taking Peggy and Andrew, leaving Little John smiling in his room by himself, at noises from the street or the house. It makes me sad, or sorry, remembering the times when he could go out with us.

215   The Life of a Special Child

April 26   Returning from the movies, we are told by Claudia that
Little John had fifteen minutes of extreme pain, his back
muscles shivering, his whole frame rigid, and piercing
screams. Since she is used to his ordinary complaining, her
sense of the extraordinary intensity of this is the more
troubling. She broke it to us very gently and cautiously, so
eager for us to have enjoyed the movies and not wanting
to spoil our evening out that I kept wanting to hug her.
John came in, tears in his eyes.

"Don't cry for Little John," I said.

"No, I'm crying because Claudia is so sweet."

Sunday,   Little John's days and nights have been less settled. We
April 27   have to alter his drugs almost from meal to meal; he's
been sicking up at bedtime, so we are feeding him a little
earlier, and then just enough liquid after our dinner to carry
his Noctec down. He's had some uncontrollable eyelid
flutterings; these used to be a pleasure to him, but now they
often start up first thing in the morning, his eyelids twitching and blinking furiously, and then his whole face screws
up in distress. We try holding his head still, pressing his
cheek, talking to him, but we can't stop it; it stops only
when the nervous spasm is over.

It's also getting harder to put the tube in. He starts screaming as soon as he realizes what we are doing, and he rarely
cries now without going quite rigid—John picked up his
ankle the other day, and his whole body lifted off the table
in one piece. When he cries at the tube going in, his throat
closes up, and the tube comes looping out his mouth or
coils in his throat above the esophagus, and we discover it
only when the milk won't go down. It's almost as much
strain as it was when we first began tube-feeding.

May 2   Today Andy went over to Little John and picked up his

216   And Say What He Is

hand the way Peggy does and moved it around. Little John began to smile, so Andrew moved it more, and John began laughing. Andrew grew more and more excited, and moved the hand so wildly we had to intercede, but it was lovely to see. He too can help with Little John, and he was exulting in it.

Sunday, May 4

Little John cried *every two minutes all day long,* after waking us up a great deal during the night. Didn't really believe he could keep it up all day, but he did.

*

He was cranky almost all last night—Emily up to him countless times—and yesterday, and the night before, with a stubborn cold. We stagger through the day.

9:00 P.M.

His annoyance so strong it wakes him screaming over his sleeping medicine given at seven. Emily is weathering this with equanimity, amazingly. She is dialing on the telephone, "It's Mrs. Murray here. I'd like to talk to Dr. Riordan." But he isn't to be reached, out of town, and the other doctor, who doesn't know Little John at all, can suggest only a nonprescription cough medicine, which we would have to drive five miles to get, and which might not help anyway, and which we doubt that Little John could swallow even if it would help.

Monday, May 5

A terrible morning, Little John screaming all the time. Dr. Riordan came and gave him a tranquilizer shot at lunchtime, which knocked him out for the afternoon.

9:00 P.M.

Impossible hours with Little John still grinding and yelling, despite a second shot from Dr. Riordan at seven. Emily has gone to bed, her stomach upset. How can she endure it? Little John coughs again, hard, after Claudia has calmed

217 The Life of a Special Child

him, and the cough triggers a renewed bout of screaming. I can't describe the sound: at an angry, sliding pitch that goes louder very suddenly, strangles, coughs, halts, then comes on again even higher and louder. It repeats, not quite regularly. It cuts right through the thick walls and doors into whatever I am trying to do.

10:30 P.M. Another bout of angry crying. He is *aware,* all too aware, of his stuffed-up nose, the mucous in his throat, the coughing. He is yelling, "GOD DAMN IT, SOMEBODY BETTER *DO* SOMETHING ABOUT THIS!"

11:10 P.M. Little John letting loose with *voiced* screams, horrifying in their suddenness and their so clearly almost worded anguish. Not helpless but yelling for help. Immensely distressing. If this night continues like this—?

Tuesday, May 6 Well it does, and I share it with Emily, and we get a number of broken hours of sleep.

*

Up fifteen times or so, between 11:30 P.M. and 2:00 A.M., every ten or fifteen minutes. So tired I would sleep in the intervals. Finally gave him Noctec rectal suppositories, which he squeezed out. Gave him Thorazine by mouth, only fairly effective; he still needed rocking. Dr. Riordan came by this morning to check him, stayed for a chat. Worried about Little John's circulation. His day off. He's a great support.

*

Dr. Johannson, a vascular surgeon, sent by Dr. Riordan, feels the pulses in Little John's legs carefully and discovers no signs of circulatory defect. He has unusually wide, flat thumbs, ideal for touching these deep pulses.

Little John keeps clenching and grinding all morning.

10:45 P.M. He has been quiet this evening, most of the time since dinner, in his rented hospital bed, big and chrome in his little room. He had outgrown his crib and could scrape his feet on the sides of it, so this, though ugly, is a temporary expedient. Emily has gone to sleep while she can, and we have some hopes Little John is getting over his cold.

Wednesday, May 7 After a night that wasn't quite so bad, I was sure his cold was really better at last, even though he was waking and screaming still. But a terrible morning again. Just after the tube went in, he had a massive nosebleed; after a minute blood was pouring down both nostrils, his mouth and throat full of it. It stopped at last when we calmed *him,* rather than trying to stop the flow of blood. He and we were very shocked. He was way back there again, distraught all morning, until Dr. Riordan came. This afternoon he really did improve in color and spirits, but I still feel shaken.

Thursday, May 8 Little John is back! His first smile for a week, and he laughed when John held him in his arms. Not an easy day— he got crosser as it went on—but at least we felt he was listening to us. Took movies putting him to bed, soothing him as he started to cry, and kissing him good-night.

Sunday, May 11, Mother's Day Very much a mother with this great brood and the hard week that has passed. Today we celebrated: a tennis racket, a new dining table delivered, which John and the girls had to carry up the precipitous driveway, and the girls cooked the first dinner to put on it as a Mother's Day present.

Monday, May 12 If the thought of losing him has made every happy moment inexpressibly sweeter and every unhappy one taut with

219 The Life of a Special Child

tragic intensity, is he not, in this way as in others, making quintessential what is inherent in ordinary life? Ought not every moment to be like this, when we consider the shortness of life? Yet how can it be? This is special, exceptional, by definition. Ordinary children *should* not give us so much joy, or such deep sorrow.

Tuesday, May 13

In bed all day with a bad back, reading for next week's seminar, Little John in bed in the next room. Telephone. Emily is talking to a woman Dr. Riordan has referred to us, the mother of a girl with a nervous system disorder not unlike Little John's. We may have suggestions, advice, or, at least, an understanding that most people can't have.

Wednesday, May 14

Beautiful classes: seminar on Willa Cather's *Death Comes for the Archbishop,* and, in poetry class, the students talked with remarkable understanding about Donne's "Death be not proud" and Shakespeare's "Poor soul the center of my sinful earth."

Thursday, May 15 7:00 A.M.

Emily up to Little John, who was crying. Changed him, back to bed. He cried for a while and stopped.

8:05 A.M.

Emily out of bed to Little John. Screaming, *"John, John"* (for me). *"He's thrown himself out of bed. I don't know if he's even alive."*

*

It seemed he was standing up at the side of the bed. In fact he was hanging, his feet touching the carpet and his jaw caught on one of the safety rails, clamping his mouth shut so he could not cry out. Perhaps the shock stopped his breathing. His eyes were closed, and his face was peaceful, though deathly white. John ran for Gina, who tried to resuscitate him, but it was much too late. Dr. Riordan came up, within three minutes of our phoning him. "Your little boy has passed on, Emily." He called the undertaker for us, and then took Peggy and Andrew off to have breakfast with Gina, so that they would not be here when the body was taken away.

A dry sick horror. Yet when I kissed him, his hair still smelled the same, only fainter. Not entirely taken from us. How one hates to part with even the dead body. For a little it seems still him.

So frail his hold on life. To think that if I had gone in to soothe him instead of lying down again, exhausted, he would still be alive. Strangely, as I lay in bed half-dozing, I was recalling times in his life when he had fallen. Why didn't those images make me get up and check?

*

The *waves* of grief rise and fall. Rising, they raise us to the crests of acceptance and understanding. Falling, they drop us into the troughs, in which we drift with our thoughts of "Couldn't we have gone in at the time it happened?"

Is there any use in thinking it out? What we are trying to keep in mind is the voyage, the whole journey, not the shock, the rough waters, the shipwreck, at the end.

Emily is crying in another room. "It's the *way* he died. It just doesn't seem possible. We were always so careful. We always met his needs. He was so vulnerable. How could we have failed him so?"

*

Peggy told Jami, who told us, "He's gone away because

they're sick, just like the little dog in the garden, and he's buried, and they can't come back, even though they want to. But the nurses and doctors can visit there."

Jami: "Really?"

Peggy: "No."

Dr. Riordan said when he brought the children back, "He achieved so much! Why, some people don't achieve anything in their whole lives, and he achieved so much in just six years!"

Claudia said, "I'm just so glad I've known him."

Cables to New Zealand and Scotland: LITTLE JOHN DIED SUDDENLY FUNERAL SATURDAY

*

Only two nights ago, standing by his bed with Jami, I had talked of what we would do if we lost Little John. I had remarked on his beauty and how one could study his face without fear or wanting to turn away, and had seen two tears on her cheeks. And Claudia and I had talked in similar ways only last night. We saw him sneer, curling up his nose as he had not done for a while, and Claudia had laughed, "That really cracks me up."

Yesterday, though he cried quite a bit, he gave us some very beautiful smiles, and one that was blinding. I came into the room and spoke teasingly, and had a sudden intense feeling that there was an *intelligent* response, that he understood *what* I was saying, not just the tone of my voice. It was a strange but exhilirating moment. Even this morning, he was still beautiful, and we were able to look at him without fear. We took Peggy in to his room to say good-bye. Later, she said, "I think Little John didn't hear me when I said good-bye?"

Since his illness he had remained troubled, his life had

narrowed down—yesterday we didn't even take him out of his bedroom. He cried a lot and fiercely, arching his body; he was so violent, it was hard not to fear for the future. The happy times have been fewer since the Easter vacation, the screaming more frequent, and not always explicable.

6:00 P.M. Alternating waves of relative calm and acute pain all day, forgetfulness and remembrance, surrounded and supported by love, friends coming by.

Rosalie stayed for a while and was very comforting. She feels a calm about him, a feeling so strong and positive about all his happiness with us that she managed to make us feel it too. She puts his life into perspective, for when she looked after him, he was much more capable, and these last years can be seen more truthfully against the years when she was with us.

Yet we are all stunned. It seems an awful way for his life to end, though the suddenness was better than a slow disintegrating illness. One friend said, "His whole life was an illness."

**Friday,
May 16** Little John says, *"Be quiet. Be at peace."* In the night I thought, these are words we can say to ourselves, speaking in his spirit on many occasions and in many forms of phrase, as a way of keeping his spirit with us.

The horror of his actual manner of dying is a truth, a fact that has to be faced. *But it is not the highest truth about Little John.*

*

One goes about the business of attending to the dead, and it is in some strange way quieting. The details of the funeral are something to do. We will have Dr. Fowler of the Presbyterian Church to give a small service. Yesterday we told him

223   The Life of a Special Child

about Little John, whom he had never met or heard about, trying to say how much this child without intellect had taught us about what is truly human. Tonight we went to the mortuary. It was strangely easing, in a room that had no connection with him at all, just as the plain wooden casket held only his body, not himself, and the face bore an expression, not really his, of slight exasperation.

Saturday, May 17

We both were *driven* awake at 4:00 A.M. So we pulled ourselves up and slowly prepared for the day, tidied the house, swept the driveway, laid out our clothes. I gathered flowers, mostly rosebuds in all sorts of soft shades, and the sharp-scented lemon verbena, some maidenhair, a few sprigs of rosemary, and made five tight posies, which I carried all together.

*

The service was to *honor* Little John, and it did. More than forty people were present, including ourselves. Bill, after getting hold of his voice, read the poem "For Little John, Approaching Three," firmly. The minister spoke eloquently, first a few of the old rolling phrases from the King James Version, "I am the Resurrection and the Life. . . . This is a house built without hands. . . . Jesus said, 'Suffer the little children to come unto me, for of such is the Kingdom of Heaven.' " And then, with enormous daring, he held Little John's name before us again like a sacrament: "Just as God has shown us, in Jesus Christ, a love greater than any human love, so in Little John He has shown us a love greater . . . than any we can know in normal life." We each left him our little bouquets to close the ceremony and make it our own. Four minutes at most and it was over.

The children were with us through it all, as they have

224   And Say What He Is

always been. They did not even notice the coffin, it was so small and plain, and covered with flowers—one spray from the New Zealand family, another from Scotland, a third from ourselves, and the fourth from a man at the florist's whom we had sheltered from the rain one night at the beach house when his truck broke down as he was delivering flowers next door.

Little John's grave lies between a huge old oak and an even older, vaster cypress in whose trunk is embedded a gravestone dated 1869. As we left, going home to a lunch with many of our friends, the sun was beginning to push through the morning fog.

*

Everything is untrue that we have thought and written about Little John's manner of dying. At the house, Dr. Riordan, who had been at the funeral, sought me out. "There is something I have to tell you, Emily. I've heard the initial results of the autopsy. There was no choking, no vomiting, no aspiration."

I said, "But if I had gone, I could have prevented him from falling."

"No. It was *agonal.* Do you know what that means? It is the movement of death, throwing the head from side to side, and the body."

"But if I had got up while he was crying, then he would not have fallen through the bars, I could have stopped it happening."

"I'm not getting through to you. He *died.* He did not *fall.*"

"You mean he died before he fell?"

"That's what I'm trying to tell you, Emily. He didn't choke, or vomit, or struggle; he died, and his body was thrown out of bed by the agonal movement, the death throes."

I asked if he was sure. "Emily, it's a fact I'm telling you; I'm not telling you something to make you feel better. The autopsy showed that he died—he didn't fall."

I cried, and then he cried too. And then the resurrection began. I said, "Oh, that does make me feel so much better."

"It makes me feel better, too. He died in the morning with the birds up, in his bed, at home—what could have been better?"

So that's why he did look so peaceful, eyes closed, in perfect sleep. And we are at peace.

We have an extraordinary sense of him still, blessing us, no longer with his smiles or indirect chuckles, but like the pool of silence, golden, filling and gathering even in the habitation of dragons.

After the funeral, birds hopped freely in and out of the dining room, picking up crumbs, fearless, and a king snake looped his splendid way past the windows.

This morning, the French door of Little John's room had blown open, as if, at last, his spirit was free to come and go, no longer tied to his body or his bed. And friends keep coming, surrounding us with tokens of love and support and of respect for Little John's life.

Afterthoughts and Images

Two gently elegiac days with Mani here. She slept in Little John's room—arrived and settled firmly into it as if to perform a special ritual, to purify it of the presence of death.

*

Dr. Riordan came by for a few minutes. "You know, it's funny. I've never felt about a child I've cared for the way I felt about Little John, and I couldn't even talk to the little fellow!"

*

Peggy: "Little John used to cry. Why did he cry? He cried because he couldn't smell things, he couldn't play with toys that he wanted, he couldn't stand up or sit or walk, he couldn't climb up and turn a tap on, Mummy!"

*

"I have a kind of memory of Little John which is part real, part imagination. I can see him, smiling, in some part of the house where light comes in through a window against a background of the darker recesses of the house. His hair is blond and delicate, his skin pale—and seems to exude light."—A friend who saw him only once.

*

Peggy asked again, "Am I going to die?"
"No, not until you are very old."
"I will be buried when I am old?"
"Grandpa is very old, and he is not buried, and we hope he will live a long time."
"Little John is buried in the ground, and he can't smile any more."

*

I think we had forgotten about death since Denver. Until then we always looked for it, but afterward we felt he was invincible. And yet, when I look back in our diaries, I see that what we were recording in the last six weeks is full of an unconscious awareness of his dying.

*

Two months: We are already so far from him! Yet also, we can think: All this effort put into living without him, all this restlessness, jumpiness, wakefulness, dodging about, and only *two months* of the rest of our lives have been burned away?

*

Peggy: "I miss taking care of Little John."
"Yes, I do too. It makes me sad."
"But you took care of him lots of times!"—as if this were a comfort. And so it was.

*

There is no special word for the parent who has lost a child, no single root, like *widow* or *orphan.* That's a gap, a hole in the lexicon—a blank wall looking onto a hidden part of the garden.

*

We ordered the grave markers. There was a quiet decent sympathy about the man who makes them. We will mark the first baby's grave, now moved beside Little John's, with our surname and her one date. On Little John's we will set one line, slightly altered, from the poem that had been written just before his birth and that seemed so close to our feelings just after he died:

His deepest griefs are healed.

*

I asked Andrew, "Do you remember Little John?"
"Yes, and Mani."
"We'll go and see Mani some time, but she lives a long way from here."
"See Mani and see John."
"No, John has died, we can't see him any more."

229   The Life of a Special Child

"He's gone."
"Yes, he's gone."

*

A sense the other night of Little John's bodily presence so
sharp and warm the tears came. Savage tears, which I welcomed because they were unasked-for, unbidden. They
proved him still present, the very moment of discovering
his death still immediate, the anguish as fierce as in those
first days when we would hold onto each other many times
a day and keep our eyes on each other so that neither of us
might wander off alone, to break down without comfort.

*

We were busy with our tax man when, noting the number
of exemptions we could claim for 1969, we had to tell him
that Little John had died. He fell silent, his pencil stopped,
amid all the sheets and folders of clients and under the
room-length shelves of *Tax-Case Decisions.* Here was the
real thing, we were all reminded, and the rest of this is
just a game—though some men's lives are spent almost
wholly in playing it.

*

To feel great sorrow, we need first to have felt an equal
joy.

*

Peggy, explaining to Andrew about making a wish when
you blow out birthday candles: "You should wish for an
ice-cream cone. A wish is something you want, but you
think about it in your head—you don't say it out loud. I'm
not going to get my wish, because it was for Little John to
come back, and he's dead and he's going to be dead for
ever and ever."

Then to me, "When I wish for Little John, he's in my head;
I'm thinking about him."

"Yes," I said, "so you *do* get your wish, in a way, because he's there in your head."

"When I remember him, I have pictures of him in my head."

I told her it was generous of her to wish for Little John to come back.

"Well," she answered, "I might make *that* wish almost all the time, but *sometimes* I might wish for an ice-cream cone."

*

That he should have lived long enough to make his point—that was how long Little John lived. Not so long as to have made it redundantly, nor so short that it would not have had time to be tested, and proved.

*

Dr. Riordan dropped by with the complete autopsy report. They found "diffuse atrophy of the cerebral cortex." The demyelinization was not general, but secondary to the atrophy. Some areas of the cortex were completely normal. There was a loss of neurons in the chain of cells—empty spaces where there should have been cells. The cerebellum was normal, and so was the brain stem. "Lots of anomalies, but nothing they could grasp on to as one main cause. He was an enigma to the pathologists."

In May of 1970, we thought that the traditional year of mourning had ended the hardest stage of our grief. But as more time passed, we could see that the depression, the discontent, the tears so quick to flow from small reminders continued. The present was the past with its center gone, always to be contrasted against the fullness of that larger-than-life existence.

As more time went by, we slowly adjusted to the change. Gradually we found we no longer needed to measure the present continually against the past. Little John lived now in some deeper layer of our minds, ineradicable. We would never be unmarked by him, but our daily life need no longer be patterned and pieced with recollections of his. We had moved on, as we had to, to the eruptions, exasperations, and satisfactions of a life with healthy, ordinary children. It is much less ordered and controlled than our life with Little John. Yet from time to time we see glimpses in their being of the sacramental significance that was daily present in his, and we are grateful.

*

for we have heard the gentlest flame
of flesh that could be   burn all night
all day   whose slender nimble light
carries yet further his brief name

under the wind-swift tinder air
we touch   our breath feeds like a wick
the moon jumps over the candlestick
the dark is weaker than a prayer